# CHILDREN'S STORY:

## Sexually Molested Children In Criminal Court

by Judge Sandra Butler Smith

Launch Press
P.O. Box 31491
Walnut Creek, CA 94598
(415) 943-7603

Library of Congress Catalog Card Number 87-82077
International Standard Book Number 0-9613205-2-4

**Thanks to:**

Minnalouooke O'Higgens, Esq.

——Rhetorician——

——or——

——pointer-up of sense and style——

Joy Rubey

——worker of endless computer magic——

.. General Thanks To:

Consuelo Callahan, Esq.

Patricia Dixon, M.D.

Beverly James, L.C.S.W.

Leila Monscharsch, Esq.

Maria Nasjettli, L.C.S.W.

Millicent Rudd, Esq.

David Wellenbrock, Esq.

"I told my mom what he was doing to me when she was gone. Mom listened. I hoped she would make it stop. She asked me if I had ever told anyone else. I told her I hadn't. She said if I ever did, I'd have to move on down the road. I was scared. A few nights later she came and woke me up and made me get in bed with him. She sat and watched. It hurt so much I said I had to go to the bathroom. I went to the bathroom and then ran out the door. It was cold and I didn't have any clothes on. I ran down the street and hid behind a bus. I saw them looking for me. I guess I decided to move on down the road."

Amy
Age 10
January 10, 1979

# Introduction

David and Goliath was not history's first recorded one-on-one contest. Perhaps David v. Goliath has won historical recognition because of the disparity in the size and power of the participants. This same disparity is found in almost every case of child molestation. The most noticeable feature of this crime is the mismatch between offender and victim. The abuser is bigger, stronger, more experienced, better at verbal skills, and holds all the power in the relationship. The child-victim is small, weak, naive, inarticulate, and powerless.

As the Israelites watched David venture forth to do battle with Goliath they were "sore afraid." So many times, I have felt that same trepidation as I watched a small child walk to the witness stand. I have felt sickened knowing what the child, this small, weak, naive, inarticulate and powerless witness is expected to do. Without any corroborating evidence, she is to convince twelve people that her body has been violated.

I have known that Goliath was waiting for her with all the weapons he could muster — words, excuses, alibis, explanations, and character witnesses. And yet, like the Israelites, I have watched as little David slew big Goliath. I have seen it over and over again. I have applauded the triumph of simplicity over duplicity, of directness over evasion and of naivete over sophistication.

Through all this, I have gleaned at least one kernel of wisdom. Children are the best witnesses in the world. All that is needed to turn a frightened victim into a giant-slayer is a little time, some sensitivity, and a few rocks for the sling. From every one of the hundreds of children I have worked with, I have learned something worth sharing.

# CONTENTS

# I.  CHILD MOLESTATION PARADIGM

*"...children are people too. By preparing a child to testify and allowing her to testify, the criminal justice system is handing back to her the control and power that has been taken from her."*

Children who have disclosed an act or acts of sexual molestation need not be further victimized by the court process. Those charged with the duties attendant to children in the criminal justice system can help create an atmosphere which accepts the child's limitations and maximizes the strength of a child's spontaneity. Children are unique witnesses.

In order for the child to be the best possible witness, the most useful witness in ascertaining the truth, pre-conceived and erroneous notions about sexual molestation must be discarded. To facilitate this desired result, court personnel must be willing to learn about the problem, both from a social and personal perspective. And in order to accurately hear and record the child's complaint, the listener, no matter who that person may be, should have some understanding of basic child development.

In any arena concerning human issues, there is a temptation to look for an easy formula to identify the truth or falsity of the issue. There is no such tool which will fashion the profile of a molested child or a molester. Child molestation cannot be viewed as a syndrome. A syndrome is a diagnostic tool which is used to identify a disease or a condition. There is, for example, a suicide syndrome. If one observes a friend to have certain signs (lassitude, withdrawal from friends and relatives, addictive dependency, etc.) one can conclude that the friend is a suicide risk. But the very nature of sexual molestation of children dictates pervasive attempts on the part of those involved to hide behind the cloak of normality. It would be almost impossible to identify a set of signs from which one could conclusively determine that a particular child was "at risk" in terms of sexual molestation. The best we can do here is formulate a model, a paradigm.

Statistically, the most common abuse occurs between a male guardian and a female child. Abuse, of course, can and does occur in other situations; father-son, mother-son, brother-sister, mother-daughter, uncle-niece, uncle-nephew, grandfather-granddaughter, next door neighbor-the kids next door, and so on. This book will deal primarily with the most classic variety, that is, father-daughter, but the comments, the approach, and the law apply to all molestation.

> The child is eight years old. She has been molested for the past six months by her stepfather. The child told her mother of the activity during that six month period. The mother denies such reports, and states that the little girl lies a lot. The child, on a brief visit to her grandmother, has told Grandma. The grandmother took the child to the police station where the child has been coaxed into telling a police officer. She repeated the story to a worker for Child Protective Services.

> The history, as revealed by the child, is that her stepfather has been caring for her and her five-year-old sister while her mother works from 6:00 p.m. to midnight. His regular routine was to put her sister to bed, and to take her to the bedroom shared by her mother and stepfather. He would disrobe her, fondle her genital and breast areas, expose his penis, and have her orally copulate him. Sometimes, he would orally copulate her.

> There is no physical evidence and no corroborating evidence.

Adults faced with the disclosure of sexual molestation often find reasons for denying belief, but more often, even if the child is believed, have difficulty in perceiving of such a case as a fit subject for a criminal proceeding. The following are some of the most cited reasons for these grave reservations:

1) **If her mother doesn't believe her, why should I?**
2) **Why did she wait six months to report?**
3) **There was no force used;**
4) **There is no corroborating evidence;**
5) **Even if it is true, testifying will be harmful;**

### 1) If her mother doesn't believe her, why should I?

Intra-family child molestations are often generational. Often the mother of the now reporting victim was molested as a child. The victim-child grows into the victim-adult and carries the emotional scars of her early experience into adulthood. She is often ill-equipped to deal with the trauma of reliving her victimization with her child.

There is obviously a problem with the stepfather in the posed example. For some reason, his own childhood victimization or his own need for mastery over another, he has chosen to sexualize a relationship with a child.

In this dysfunctional framework, there grows between the woman and the man a silent agreement to ignore some rather substantial problems within the relationship. In short, the child is the unfortunate recipient of each parties problems.

The mother's involvement in or knowledge of the molestation is as varied as the occurrences. Some mothers actually participate in the assaults. Some stand by passively even though aware of the assaults on their children. Some remain silent from fear, either for themselves or their children. Some do know of the abuse, but do not let themselves acknowledge it on any conscious level, and still others actually are totally unaware of the child's predicament.

In our example, the mother should have known of the abuse, but would not allow herself to consciously acknowledge it. She had come home on a couple of occasions unexpectedly from work and found the child in the bed she and her husband shared. The stepfather was hurriedly trying to put the child's clothes back on. The mother, denying her own victimization, denies the abuse of her child. It becomes the family secret.

Some mothers side with the man and do everything possible to undermine the child. Some mothers of victims attempt to convince the child that the responsibility for the sexual activity rests on the shoulders of the child. Some turn against the child and actively participate in the defense of the molester. Some seek to convince the child that she is responsible for the economic survival of the family.

A woman raised in an abusive family is hard-pressed to know how to deal with the trauma occasioned by her child's victimization. Having been powerless in much of her life, and suffering from what is often called the pattern of "learned helplessness" she will probably be unable, initially, to offer any support, strength, or power to her child.

To add a measure of balance, it is also important to note that many mothers immediately believe the child's disclosure and stand by the child through thick and thin. This kind of support is the most effective determinant of a child's successful passage through any trauma, whether a court process or an emotional upheaval.

# CHILD MOLESTATION PARADIGM

The ideal system would immediately offer services to all members of the family. The mother would receive counseling, support, and instruction in dealing with her own feelings as well as those of her child. The prosecutor can play a part in this rehabilitative program by encouraging the mother to support the child throughout the court process. To this end, the prosecutor ought to make the mother understand the process of the court and the importance of supporting the child. She should be told what to expect at every stage of the proceedings. Her denial is often only her first reaction. Time and concern by those around her may result in putting it aside. The mother can be an invaluable asset to a prosecutor's case. She should be treated as one.

Keeping the child safe and free of possible molestation begins at the arraignment stage for the prosecutor. The contemporaneous juvenile proceedings do not insure that the child will be kept safe from the molestation. Juvenile court cannot keep a child out of the home simply because there is a possibility that the family might try to influence the child. In many cases, if the mother has not overtly participated in the sexual activity, the child will remain with her. An unconditionally released defendant is free to pressure his way back into the home and a position of power over the victim-child. Therefore, in criminal court the prosecutor must seek to ensure a neutral atmosphere for the victim-child during the pendency of the proceedings. Whether the defendant is released on bail, or on his own recognizance, a stay-away, no-contact order must be sought as a condition of either bail or O.R. A conditional O.R. release is preferable to bail with no conditions, for if the child finds herself back in the family setting, the opportunities for the adult participants to pressure her are staggering. These children have been taught to assume a responsible, adult role within the family, and under very little pressure, will recant and seek to protect the adults.

Such was the case with three little girls, ranging in age from eight to thirteen, who were molested by their father for years. He subjected them to oral copulation, intercourse, and sodomy. Once again, it came to light when the thirteen-year-old wanted to date. Father refused and in anger, she told her mother of the sexual activities between the girls and their father. Mother reported it to the police, primarily because she wanted out of the marriage. Because she was the one who reported, the children

4

were left in her custody. The father, out on his own recognizance, returned frequently to the home. When the mother discovered the possibility of Daddy going to prison, she, along with the father, pressured the children not to testify. Her efforts were successful and the three girls appeared in court and refused to answer questions. Despite the pleading of the prosecutor and the warning of the judge, they continued to refuse to answer the questions. One by one, they were held in contempt, and taken to juvenile hall where they spent the weekend — Halloween weekend. When brought back to court on Monday, they testified. They told the court that Mother had told them that if they testified, all of them and Mother would be "put out on the street". In short, the mother was willing to sacrifice her children and the children were willing to be sacrificed. They were assuming responsibility for the other family members.

## 2) Why did she wait six months to report the incident?

Why don't children report these incidents immediately? Why is it that molestation will often go on for years? Those cases seen and investigated by policing agencies are just the tip of the iceberg. Many, many women reach adulthood without ever revealing their childhood molestation to anyone. Incest is a subject very seldom mentioned in polite company. Victims of sexual molestation are often deeply shamed and find very few safe opportunities to discuss their intimate sexual secrets.

Victims remain silent for a variety of reasons. The most obvious is fear. "If you tell anyone, I'll kill your little sister". "If you tell, I'll have to go to jail and you won't have any place to live, or any food to eat." "If you tell, I'll kill myself." It is surprising how many molesters will employ this last threat, but it is not surprising how effective it is in silencing a child. Children tend to be magical thinkers, that is, they will assume responsibility. Often in divorces, the child assumes responsibility. "If I had been a better daughter, this would not have happened". A child will often assume responsibility for the death of a loved one because, in anger, the child once wished the loved one dead. In one case in which the molesting man threatened to kill himself if the child told the secret, she did, in fact, tell and he did, in fact, kill himself. That child, now an adult, has lived in and out of the state hospitals all of her life. The child accepted responsibility for the death of the parent who abused her.

Threats are not the only means of obtaining compliance and silence. Child molesters often buy silence. "If you don't tell, I'll get you a kitten." "If you don't tell, I'll take you to Disneyland." Children, along with being magical thinkers, are also concrete and pragmatic thinkers and the *quid pro quo* seems perfectly logical to them. These pay-offs for silence are often seen by the outside world as proof of a marvelously loving and giving relationship between father and child. People will often tell the child how lucky she is to have such a devoted Daddy. The outside world is, in effect, reinforcing the molesting situation. Certainly, not all close father-daughter relationships are incestuous or molesting in nature. But the molesting relationship can be misinterpreted by well-meaning outsiders.

The child may also remain silent out of ignorance. Children have no experience by which to judge their parents' behavior. For all the five-year-old knows, Daddy's conduct is perfectly normal. The child, trapped in her tiny world, threatened or seduced into silence, will cause no problems for the molesting party for weeks, months, or even years; sometimes never at all. All the while the conspiracy of silence is creating more and more of a problem for the child. If no safe opportunity to reveal the secret presents itself to the young child, life will go on in this abnormally "normal" atmosphere. Frequently, the child becomes a teenager before realizing that not all Daddies play these games. As the child matures, she acquires sexual experience and the ability to verbalize about sex. Daddy becomes frightened. Will experience ungag the child's mouth? When the child reaches these years, the hideous spectre of "boys" rises on Daddy's horizon. Often, at that point, the family is torn apart as Daddy becomes the jealous lover. Violence erupts and molested teenage girls run away from home in droves, seeing flight as the only answer.

The parents of thirteen and fifteen-year-old sisters had been divorced for years. Mother, although living in town, did not live with them. Both girls slept with Daddy every night. The molestation of both was constant. The fifteen-year-old met a young man of sixteen at school and things developed as usual when boy meets girl. The boy come from a nice family, who, on two or three occasions, took the girl out to the movies, or to dinner with them. Daddy, a heavy drinker, harbored a growing rage at the apparent loss of one of his possessions. One evening, quite drunk, he demanded that the girl call the young man and have him come to the house. She did so, quite reluctantly, since she was well aware of her father's penchant for violence. When the boy arrived, Daddy ranted and raved at the two of them, growing progressively more violent. He then demanded that the thirteen-year-old go and get his handgun which was kept in a hall closet. The thirteen-year-old did get the gun, but had the wherewithal to remove the bullets. Daddy was furious upon the discovery of the bullets missing, and vented his anger by slapping the boy across the face with the gun, breaking a tooth. The boy later explained this away to his parents as a basketball injury. A few weeks later, again in a drunken state, Daddy demanded that the fifteen-year-old get the young man to the house. She refused, he beat her, she called, the boy came. Daddy had the gun, with bullets this time, and told them both to stand. It was clear to all present, including the thirteen-year-old, that Daddy intended to execute both the girl and her boyfriend. The thirteen-year-old, who was standing to the side, knocked the gun from his hand. The young man grabbed it and shot Daddy. The three criminals made their getaway on a ten speed bike.

This is not an atypical story. Child molestation generally ends in some kind of tragedy.

## 3) There was no force used.

Child molestation, like rape, is considered a "sex" crime. Rape cases are certainly proved more easily if the victim has injuries. Injuries corroborate the victim's testimony that the sexual acts were non-consensual. In the past, prosecutors have viewed lack of injury in a rape as a deficiency. Experience and education have proven this theory faulty.

In many "sex" cases, the offender becomes, in essence the victim's jailer. Why don't jailers use physical force? Jailers have the force of *authority* behind them. The prisoner, the rape victim, and the victim-child simply know that something bad will happen to them if they do not obey. A successful jailer so thoroughly institutionalizes his prisoners that the compliance of the one jailed is automatic.

This psychological framework makes force an unnecessary excess. Sexual activity with a child is conclusively presumed to be nonconsensual. Unlike the rape case, the defense cannot claim that the activity is consensual or that the child was the aggressor.

The differing size and power of the offender and the victim dictates that force is unnecessary and places him in an immediate position of authority. Unless the offender is heavy-handed in discipline or enjoys inflicting pain, an absence of injury indicates nothing.

Physical force is rarely used against children in order to accomplish the offender's sexual gratification. Instead, the general case presents a carefully cultivated garden of molestation. First, the seeds are planted in the child's mind. There is often a lengthy period of germination, allowing the child to accept the idea of the initial touching. After fruition, the produce is kept in a fenced, carefully weeded, and protected environment. This constant attention and protection insures that no one will get close enough to discover the family secret. These families tend to be isolated from the community. Although, the molesting family may live in an urban setting, the family remains isolated from neighbors. The only contact with the outside world is often the church.

Even if force is used, there will seldom be any evidence.

> On her tenth birthday Father took his daughter to the bedroom, and had her fill the bathtub with water. He unzipped his pants, and told her to "suck it". When she evidenced reluctance to do so, he held her head under the water until she reconsidered her position.

So many times, even when force is used, the force leaves no demonstrable evidence. All children must, of necessity, depend on adults for care, provisions, and emotional nurturing. The family unit is the whole world to the child. Molested children as well as abused children accept their treatment as the norm. As the child grows and her horizons widen, the threats or promises begin to increase in ever more desperate attempts to keep her quiet and compliant. It is generally some family upheaval that destroys the fences of silence that surround the family secret.

> One twelve-year-old ran from her home to a little friend's house when the pay-offs turned to abuse. Instead of offered trips to Disneyland, she now received physical abuse. Having learned her lessons well, she did not tell the parents of the girlfriend why she was afraid to go home, reporting only that her father was mean. These parents saw fear in the child indicative of more than

her vague references to ill-treatment. When her father appeared, wild with rage, the police were called because of his maniacal behavior. Her fear of going home finally overcame her fear of breaking the silence, and she told of years of molestation.

Many times in families with more than one girl, the oldest girl will suffer in silence as long as she thinks that she alone is being victimized. But if she sees her sisters are about to be drawn in as well, she may break the silence of years to protect them. Although children are not adept at protecting themselves, they will often protect other children.

Molestation sometimes will come to light as a result of an imminent divorce. The children or child will see the divorce as a way out. Often, the mother will signal a reconciliation. In desperation, the child finds words and a voice to tell her mother, or other family members, about her victimization.

No matter how the facts are brought to light, the offender, almost without exception, will react with anger, rage, and frantic denial. The angry reaction may later turn to a plea for sympathy, understanding and forgiveness. The family and society may rush headlong into accepting these apologies, forgetting that it is not the place of others to forgive this crime in which they were not the victim. Nor do those who hurry to put the matter behind them realize the child-victim will almost without exception try to soften the details. In part, this is because she has not dealt with the subject and has managed to repress a great deal of it for her own survival, and because she is continuing to protect the molester.

### 4) There is no corroborating evidence.

Unlike a rape case, which is frequently reported so promptly that the victim can be taken to the hospital for examination and collection of evidence, a child molestation case is often devoid of physical evidence. The last event may have occurred weeks or even months before the report. Nevertheless, it is imperative that the child be taken for a physical examination. The child will understate the incidents. She may maintain she was only fondled, but medical evidence may prove otherwise. If the story indicates a lengthy history of access to the child, she should be examined. One nine-year-old child indicated the only contact she had with a man was fondling. She maintained that story to the police and all others. A physical examination for a sore throat revealed gonorrhea of the throat. Even tiny babies are seen with herpes infections and every other venereal disease known to man and womankind.

Prosecutors should familiarize themselves with local medical facilities and with the training of doctors who most frequently handle these cases. In one county hospital in this state, which is also a teaching facility for interns and residents, the physician who headed the gynecological department actually thought babies could not get gonorrhea. He maintained this view until the head pediatrician rather dramatically disabused him on it. The pediatrician explained to him, in the presence of interns and residents, while placing the literature in front of him, that children, like adults, do not get venereal disease from sitting on dirty potties, or kissing door knobs. Babies get venereal disease in the same ways and from the same sources as do adults.

Although no examination protocol exists for suspected child molestation, the profession has made great advancements in evaluation and treatment of sexually molested children. The enormity of the problem has had profound effects on the medical profession. Certain routine approaches are now used in the examinations. The child is examined for any injuries (scrapes, bruises, tears). A special lamp is used for detecting semen. If any evidence is apparent, a "rape kit" is prepared. The mouth is examined for trauma and disease. Signs of trauma in the genitals and rectal areas are noted. There should also be a search for scarring and discharge.

Many facilities are now using colposcopes to magnify and photograph sexually abused children. The colposcope has proven to be a non-intrusive method of examination and recordation of evidence.

Medical evidence is only one type of corroborating evidence. Even though the sexual occurrences went unobserved by others, the access which the alleged perpetrator had to child may have been witnessed. Changed behavior on the part of the child may have been noted. The child might have begun to complain of strange physical maladies. This is corroboration as surely as a ruptured hymenal ring.

Although most child molestation cases lack any corroborating medical testimony, the child's account of the molest may be self-corroborating. Children do lie, but they are not good at it. Children can only make up stories within their frame of reference. A child may tell you that her favorite book was torn apart by a dog, or that a burglar came in and ripped it up. These are explanations within a child's frame of reference. If pressed for details, however, the child will let her story get out of control. Packs of ravenous dogs and maniacal monsters enter into the picture. But when pressed for details, a molested child can tell the prosecutor what a penis looks like, that sometimes it hangs down and sometimes it stands up, that white "yukky" stuff comes out of it, that it can be put in your mouth, that a hand can be put around it and moved up and down, and that it can be moved back and forth between your legs. An average eight-year-old girl cannot describe these events.

Some eight-year-olds indeed can describe such events. But here the prosecutor benefits from the little-known "presumption of innocence." If defense counsel cannot show a specific instance where the child learned of these details from friends, from pictures, or wherever, the jury will assume that she learned them in the school of experience taught by the defendant.

The ideal jury for the trial of a sexual molestation case is made up of parents. Parents bring common sense to the court,room with them. That common sense tells them that their eight-year-old daughter could not have described such events. A single credible witness is sufficient for the proof of any issue. Nothing is more credible or more winning than a child recounting events in the words and language of a child. Children need to be supported during these difficult times, but they do not need to be coached. Coaching and patronizing will destroy the most valuable asset of the child-witness, the freshness.

### 5) Even if it is true, will testifying be harmful?

A misplaced desire to protect the child sometimes results in prosecutors, police officers and other well-meaning adults treating the child like a china doll. This concern often results in not going further with prosecution. While there are some really valid reasons to not go through a court proceeding, the china doll syndrome should not be one of them. Children often reflect the affect of the adults close to them. Displays of this behavior occur frequently when parents are about to leave a small child with a baby-sitter. The child is fine until Mom and Dad start trying to reassure the child that everything is O.K. Their concern and uneasiness convinces the child that there is really something to worry about and the tantrum begins. Similarly, children in being interviewed will react to the affect of the interviewer. If the interviewer presents a shocked or angry face, the child will react to that message. She will think that she has been shamed.

On the other hand, a friendly and concerned interviewer imparts that attitude.

A noble but misguided concern serves neither the prosecutor nor the victim. The officer, prosecutor, or social worker who adopts this approach is actually inhibiting the child's cure. Anger, rage, and self-destruction result from a loss of control. Molested children have lost control over the most fundamental concept of the self: the integrity of one's body. Investigation and prosecution allow a child a safe forum from which to vent that anger and rage.

Any sensitive prosecutor has seen the fear exhibited by victims of other types of crimes. Burglary victims feel that they have lost the safety of their homes. Robbery victims feel they have lost a sense or personal security, as well as their money. Rape victims feel the loss of both the security of their homes and the privacy of their bodies. Studies have shown that rape victims whose assailants were caught and went to trial, have a much faster and more complete recovery than those victims whose assailants were never brought to trial. Children are people, too. By preparing a child to testify and allowing her to testify, the criminal justice system is handing back to her the control and power that has been taken from her.

Children need to learn that adults have no right to subject them to sexual activity. They need to be taught that there is something that they, even as children, can do to make it stop — talk. Children change from frightened little mice to happy, assertive little kids when they discover that they need not continue to be victims. Dramatic changes occur in children in a very short period of time. One eight-year-old who could only cry into the shoulder of the social worker at her first meeting with the prosecutor, was so confident and secure by the end of the trial that she laughingly told the prosecutor that she was going to give the defendant a weenie roaster for his birthday.

Sexual molestation cases are hardly glamorous. Counties with an aggressive approach to prosecution find that the incidence of sexual molestation and exploitation of children is rampant. In some counties, policing agencies loathe to investigate child molestation, but experience shows that this attitude generally stems from a lack of education in the area, and also from a belief on the part of the policing agency that such cases will not be prosecuted. Prosecution and law-enforcement should present a united front in the attack on this overwhelming problem. Officers and prosecutors should train and work together. Prosecutors should keep the officers apprised of the law, and the officers should actively acquaint prosecutors with the problems faced by them in the investigation. Each agency should be willing to listen to the needs of the other in order to present a cohesive approach.

Aggressive prosecution of child molestation cases will result in a significant increase in the number of cases filed. One county went from 3 reported cases in January of 1978 to 35 reported cases in January of 1979. With one in every four girls suffering from molestation in one form or another, and one in every nine boys, the potential case load is staggering. The good news in these statistics is that after a number of successful prosecutions many of the later cases can be resolved short of trial. The prosecutor's confidence in dealing with the case and with the child will effect an early disposition of the case.

Our society has ended slavery, unchained children from machines, and taken children out of the mines. A determined society can surely make significant inroads on the problem of sexual exploitation of children.

# CHILDREN'S STORY

# II.    INVESTIGATION

*...with a little compassion the officer can show the child that not she but "Daddy", is the freak."*

Most criminal cases have the decency and sense of fair play to hint that a crime has been committed. The corpus delicti makes a rather major statement: a dead body, a robbed store, a frightened and angry rape victim. Child molestation cases, on the other hand, leave only faint clues. The trial of the molester has been carefully camouflaged. Even experienced people will sometimes overlook the signs that mark the passage of a molester through a child's life.

Child molestation cases become public by varied and circuitous paths.

It is imperative that policing agencies teach their officers some basic facts about sexual molestation of children. Education in this area is essential because false information abounds and is accepted by most people as being truth.

## Fiction

1. Children make these stories up.
2. Children make these stories up to punish their parents.
3. It will hurt the child to dredge this up.
4. If the acts did occur it was just the father's way of expressing love.
5. The child "asked for it."
6. It's a family matter.
7. It only happens among lower income families.
8. The kid is out of the house now, it's best to leave it alone.
9. Law enforcement has more important things to concentrate on.
10. So what, there's no harm done.

# INVESTIGATION

1. When the subject of child molestation first came into public view, the early pioneers in the area often were heard to say that children don't lie. The point of that statement was to dispel earlier misconceptions that these disclosures were always or nearly always the product of an over-active imagination. As time passed, it became apparent that such a statement was much too simplistic. Of course children lie. Teenagers lie. Adults lie. No age group has a corner on the lying market. What is apparent, however, is that the sophistication of lies often improves with age.

   Most small children do not have enough information to fabricate a convincing and coherent story about sexual acts. As they grow older, obviously, the index of sexual information has grown so the ability to weave sexual facts into a story grows. But as a child approaches puberty, the shame connected with sex also increased, so talking about it or admitting to any kind of sexual contact becomes more difficult.

   Credibility of any witness or victim is something which must be evaluated. The credibility of children is also in question. That is why it is so necessary to judge the child's statement against the background to what is known of normal childhood development.

2. Once again, the ability of a child to punish his or her parents is directly related to how sophisticated that child is. Small children may wish their parents dead. This is the child's very concrete way of imagining evening up the score for a parental transgression, real or imaginary. Angry small children throw tantrums and call their parents names.

   As the child matures, the science of torturing parents matures. They swear, they wear inappropriate clothes, they may drink and even experiment with drugs, but rarely would they report being sexually abused, because, in the youngster's mind such an act also says something shameful about him or her. First, it is an admission that one does not come from a "good family", and second it shames the child.

3. Perhaps, the most damaging aspect of child molestation is the secrecy in which it is cloaked. Children should be open, spontaneous and free.

# CHILDREN'S STORY

Children are not injured by having their lives made decent and normal. They are injured by not being allowed the power to control their own bodies. The harm is in the silence, not in the speaking.

4. Sexual exploitation of children is not love and there should never be any confusion about that. The love of a parent for a child is caring and giving; the ultimate goal is to produce an independent adult. A molested child has been raised in an atmosphere of lies, manipulation, and exploitation. This atmosphere has nothing to do with love. The father's motive is his own sexual gratification, not concern for the welfare of his child.

5. The child cannot "ask for it". The law says that children under the age of 18 are incapable of consent. The molester and family members supporting the molester frequently regale officers with tales of the child's promiscuous nature. Promiscuous children do exist and the source of that promiscuity lies in the home. If the child is exhibiting sexual behavior, it is because he or she has learned that such behavior can be used to secure "love" and attention. The fault is not the child's.

6. This is not a family matter. If the perpetrator of such a crime were a stranger to the child, people would not take such a cavalier attitude. Though stranger danger is certainly a concern, the potential for continued traumatization is greater in the intrafamilial situation. Unhappy and powerless children become unhappy and powerless adults. Sexual "family matters" do not stay in the home.

The effects of intrafamilial molestation have serious implications for all society. Molested girls often grow into adulthood filled with self-loathing. Since nothing about our society condones violence in girls and women, they often follow a self-destructive path. These women fill our jails charged with what are commonly known as victimless crimes. They fill their bodies with drugs, both legal and illegal. They support this destructive way of life through prostitution.

Young men, on the other hand, are given permission to act out in more violent ways. These former victims may later become the people we fear most—rapists, murders, robbers, and just to bring it full circle, child-molesters.

Society has a price to pay for this "family matter".

7. The latest figures available indicate that at least a tenth of our population was molested in some form as children. The victims and the victimizers were representative of all classes, cultures, and races. All children are vulnerable. The difference in the numbers of reported cases where criminal juvenile court prosecution is sought is more reflective of the ability of the perpetrator to cover his tracks and buy out of exposure than being an accurate reflection of incidence.

8. The removal of the child from the home does not necessarily solve the problem. Families, particularly the molester, frequently race to set up a seemingly safe situation for the child. The molester proclaims his responsibility and his intentions to seek help immediately. If law enforcement accepts the outward signs as the answer to the problem, the safety of the child will often be temporary and the counseling brief. Only time will tell if the molester is sincere. Counseling is a long, painful process that few endure freely. The offender must face the legal consequences of his acts.

9. If the ultimate goal of law enforcement is to make our streets and homes safe, there is no greater contribution to this end than the protection of children. Abused and molested children are the seeds; rapists, murderers, robbers, drug addicts, burglars, prostitutes and more child abusers are the fruit. A society reflects the treatment of children.

10. The harm to the individual child is personal and profound. The scars are not as visible as those found on a physically abused child, but they are often just as damaging. A child raised in an atmosphere where every trust has been violated grow to adulthood unable to connect with another person in an open caring, and responsible relationship. Without radical intervention and therapeutic treatment, some of these children are crippled for life.

The education of law enforcement officers should be continuing. The problems and prevalence of child molestation is only beginning to be explored. There are techniques which can be learned to make handling the situation easier on the officer and on the child-victim.

## DO'S

1. Get out from behind the desk.
2. Get down to the child's physical level.
3. Chat about other things first.
4. Be open, friendly and playful.
5. Treat the child as you would any child.
6. Treat the subject matter-of-factly.
7. Take the lead in asking questions.
8. Get as detailed as possible.
9. Look carefully at the safest place for the child to be placed.
10. Assure the child that this is not her fault.

## DON'T'S

1. Don't use big words.
2. Don't act as if this situation is surely going to ruin her life.
3. Don't hide behind a desk.
4. Don't act shocked or dismayed.
5. Don't jump to the conclusion that she hates the molester.
6. Don't neglect interviews of the entire family.
7. Don't be afraid of the words or subject matter.
8. Don't give up if there is some initial resistance.
9. Don't get angry.
10. Don't ever doubt a small child who tells you she has been the victim of these activities.

Obviously, the majority of money, time and effort should be spent on the training of juvenile officers. However, all officers should receive some training regarding child molestation, the warning signs, and some simple techniques for dealing with the situation. Realizing how common child molestation is, it will be clear that every officer is going to have to deal with a case of several cases or a host of cases of molestation during the course of his or her career.

Patrol officers are asked to respond to a variety of situations. In each situation, the officer is expected to adapt his or her skills and intellect to the problem at hand. Law enforcement demands some very human qualities. Walking unsuspectingly into a child molestation case demands an open and alert mind. The most insidious aspect of this type of case is the speed with which a seemingly routine call can turn into a volatile problem.

What started out as a dispatch on a kidnapping turned into a full blown child molestation investigation. A neighborhood mother called, frantically screaming that her son and two other children had been kidnapped off the street by a man a couple of blocks away. He was holding them in the house and a would not let them out. The frantic mother intimated that there might be a gun involved. Patrol was dispatched immediately. Upon arrival at the house, the officers were able to talk to the man through the closed door. He announced that these three boys had done something "awful" to his daughter and he was "going to teach them a lesson they'd never forget." The officers called for a juvenile division back up and after approximately an hour, the combined efforts of patrol and juvenile officers won the release of the three thoroughly shaken teenagers.

Patrol questioned the father (kidnapper). Father indicated he had caught these boys pulling down the pants of his eleven-year-old daughter and he was going to scare them to make sure they never did such an awful thing again. He assured patrol that there was no gun and allowed them to look around the house. There was, in fact, no gun. He promised that it was all over and all was forgiven.

In the meantime, the juvenile officers were talking to the three bad boys. The boys admitted to pulling down the little girl's pants and did think that at 14 they were probably a bit old to be engaging in such aberrant behavior. They promised never to do it again.

Reason triumphed and the matter was handled in just a little over two hours. The officers, both patrol and juvenile, rightly pleased with their deft handling of the situation, went on about their business. One hour later, the same patrol officers were dispatched back to the house of the formerly frantic woman and her formerly kidnapped son. Upon arrival they learned the following: that Mother, being a mother after all, had not been quite so easy on the young man as the officers. She was bound and determined to get to the bottom of this totally unacceptable behavior. The young man finally copped a plea, but told her that he thought he had a defense. It seems that the older brother of the little girl had told these boys that his Dad took off the girl's clothes every night and did things to her and had her do things to him. With well-known teenage reasoning powers, this boy and his buddies decided that if it was O.K. for her old man then it was O.K. for them. Those same teenage reasoning powers failed to warn them that Daddy might be jealous of his "property." And so the foregoing events occurred.

The patrol officers received this information, coaxing the boy just a bit along the way. They undoubtedly got more information than his mother did because he was interviewed out of her presence. Patrol then called for juvenile officers and met them back at the scene of the crime. When Daddy opened the door, he was told that there was, perhaps, more to the problem than had been expected. The woman juvenile officer asked to speak to the little girl and the man juvenile officer asked to speak to the older brother. The uniformed officers stood by, chatting with Daddy about football scores and fishing.

The little girl, who was being interviewed in the kitchen, originally denied that her father had ever "bothered" her. The juvenile officer informed her that her brother had told the boys who had given her the trouble in the afternoon that things had been going on between her and her father. She still maintained a stoic denial. The turning point came when the officer took her hands and said, "I'm going to make it stop if you'll just tell me." The little girl dissolved into tears and whispered, "Yes, he bothers me." With some calm, assuring, and sympathetic, but not patronizing questions, the officer finally got some pertinent facts from the child. She told the officers that for the past three years, her father had been "putting his thing in my thing." Before he had just "fooled around" with her.

Meanwhile, in the bedroom, older brother was proving a much tougher nut to crack. Initially, he refused to talk to the officer at all. When confronted with the statement of the other young boy, he denied ever saying such a thing. After a conference with the woman officer who had interviewed the girl, the boy still denied knowing anything. The turn‚around came when the officer told him that this was going to be his last chance to help his little sister. If he didn't say what he knew now, she was going to be taken from the home, he would be left and she would have to face this uncertain future by herself. He then wanted to know what was going to happen if he told them what he knew. The officer replied, "We're going to make it stop." After a few minutes, the boy admitted that he had walked in on his sister and father in his parents' bedroom on one occasion and found his father "humping" her. He would not admit to any more than this.

Both children were then taken to the station in the police car. The parents were told that the children were being taken into protective custody and that they would be contacted later. (In this case, the parents, though they protested, did not attempt to interfere. Sometimes, however, the fight will be on. Undoubtedly, the presence of two uniformed officers helped to defuse the situation.)

Once at the facility, the children were again separated and reinterviewed. As is always the case, many more facts came out. The little girl remembered the time her brother walked in on them. Through gentle and careful questioning, she was finally able to establish the date of that occurrence as sometime during the last Christmas vacation. She said that her brother was usually sent outside when things would occur and her mother would just be "out." (Later it was determined that Mommy had a boyfriend, so she was out frequently, which suited Daddy's nefarious purposes.) The officer then said, "I have some yukky questions that I have to ask you, but they are for your own good, Does it hurt when you go to the bathroom? Do you menstruate yet? Is there any yukky stuff in you panties? The girl had not started menstruation and she did not have yukky stuff in her pants and it did hurt when she went to the bathroom. ("Yukky stuff" is a wonderful phrase. Kids understand it perfectly.)

The older brother admitted to knowing what was going on. He said that he was always sent to the store or to a friend's house or just outside, but would see his sister being taken into the master bedroom. As the story unfolded, the reason for the silence of these two children became patently obvious. Daddy was an absolute dictator. Compliance with his orders had to be immediate or the kids literally were bounced off the walls. Both were scared to death of Daddy. They were then taken to the hospital for a check-up. The brother had minor bruises, nothing serious. At least he had no significant injuries to the outside of his body. The little girl, however, had a severe vaginal infection.

One of the really "wonderful" jobs associated with being a female juvenile officer is that victims will probably want her to stay in the room with them during the gynecological examination. This was probably not what was envisioned when a job in law enforcement was sought. Nor is it an aspect of duty that any member of the public would imagine or identify as "part of the job."

The two children were booked into the dependent children's home. Both officers returned to the police facility to find Mommy and Daddy waiting for them. The parents were separated, and were *Mirandized*.

It cannot be emphasized enough that the mother is always a prospective defendant in these cases, if not as an active participant, then as an aider and abettor. Steps should be taken to insure that her statement is not excluded from the court. Judges have a way of ignoring good intentions: it has never been particularly legally persuasive to say, "But I was just trying to be nice. I didn't know any better."

The Mother was interviewed by the female juvenile officer. Her initial comment, "Do you think I would have stayed with a man who did that sort of thing to my daughter?", was met by the officer's "Yes." Mother was asked, "You knew your children were afraid of him, didn't you know why?" "No," she answered. The officer then recited every gory detail, from the fondling to the intercourse to the physical abuse to the vaginal infection. "Now, I learned this from her in just a very brief time this afternoon, and you've lived with her for 11 years!" Eventually Mommy stated that she did think that the discipline was a little heavy handed, but maintained her ignorance of the molestation. She stated that she had a man-friend, and did go out a lot and leave the children with her husband. Eventually, she said that she did believe that something had happened to her daughter. The officer then worked on convincing her that her daughter needed her support and love at this time. "I know you want to do right by your daughter. Well, she needs you right now. She needs your love and concern." By telling the mother that she expected her to do the right thing, the officer may have pushed her in the direction of doing the right thing. The mother did agree to go to the hospital and be tested for the presence of the infection which afflicted her daughter. She signed releases of medical information for both herself and her daughter.

This release enables the officer or prosecutor to acquire the results of the medical examinations without a subpoena duces tecum. In most jurisdictions, the mother could be charged with some section of the laws protecting children. Practically all jurisdictions make criminal the failure to protect a child from abuse, when that abuse is known or should be known to a person in a care-taking role. It did not appear, at this point, the mother would be charged. The officers should be sure, however, that their interview is reported in great detail. Mother or other care-takers may later become witnesses, willing or reluctant, for prosecution or the defense.

The interview of Daddy was unproductive. From the onset, he denied everything. The male juvenile officer explained that the children were interviewed separately. They did not have time or opportunity to get together and make up these stories. The father was told all the gory details. He told the officer that the girl was promiscuous and that's why she said "all that stuff." He denied every touching her in anything but a fatherly manner. The officer patiently went through each of the allegations. The father angrily denied or tried to explain away each of the allegations.

This is a painstaking and seemingly futile process, but it is not fruitless. If a case gets to court, the deputy district attorney and the investigating officer must both have some idea of what the defense is going to be. During the initial interview with Daddy they can find out if the man is committed to an "I ain't guilty, I didn't do nothin'" defense. In this case, the father finally attempted to explain the child's motive to lie by saying that she had stolen $1 from him and this was her way of getting back at him. (The jury was no doubt heavily impressed by the reasonableness of this explanation.)

The suspect had no explanation for the boy's assertions. However, at this point Daddy thought he was humming right along since he had admitted nothing. The officer asked him if he would be willing to have a physical examination. The man agreed and signed a medical release. He was taken to the hospital for examination and then into the county jail.

In this example, the officers were called upon to deal with a wide variety of human behaviors. Initially they quelled a dangerous situation. They then had to cajole information from a number of uncooperative individuals. In each case, the officer adapted the approach to the situation. To have accepted the initial denial of the children would have been folly. To yell and scream at the mother would have cemented her support to the husband and turned her against her children. The patience in dealing with the father resulted in his commitment to a defense. Each participant in this drama was treated as an individual. The individual treatment resulted in a successful prosecution.

### The Runaway

Children, particularly teenagers, run away from home for a variety of reasons; drugs, dissatisfaction with the rules of home life, stupidity, peer-group pressure and so on. However, there is a growing body of evidence suggesting that a great number of the runaway girls, and possibly boys, are running from molestation in the home. There are the easily-identifiable molested girls who turn up on the streets as hookers and/or dope dealers. These youngsters will often readily admit their reason for being on the streets. Other runaways may be so disenchanted with the world and the systems which have failed them, that they would never admit the reason for their lifestyle, preferring the tough-urchin act to any hint of victimization.

An officer who picks up such a teenager should explore the possibility of molestation as the hidden reason. Many runaways come to the attention of law enforcement because of some illegal activity on their part, not because they have been reported missing by the family. That lack of a missing persons report is significant. Healthy families generally care a great deal when their children don't come home.

"Where do you come from?" "Do your parents know where you are?" "Is there some reason why you don't want to go home?" "Has someone been bothering you?" These kids are not generally the most lovable, likable, freckle-faced rascals ever encountered, and spending time with them in an effort to find out what drove them from their homes is often not pleasant. But babies aren't born bad, they're made bad. Children don't take their first steps as rotten little brats. Rotten kids come from environments which have twisted and stunted them. Although it may be too late to save the runaway child who is in trouble with the judicial system, aggressive investigation may save her brothers or sisters in the home, or neighborhood kids.

Children who appear to be hard as nails will often soften if they are asked to protect another child.

> One young lady of thirteen had lived with three of the most renowned child molesters in town. She was actually quite proud of that fact. She bragged to the officers that she had been on her own since she was eleven. She also bragged about the size of her vagina, but she would not tell the officer of any acts that occurred between herself and these three men. As the interview went on, an eight-year-old was brought in who was thought to have been with one of these men. The eight-year-old had gonorrhea of the throat. Another officer was trying to interview her across the room. The eight-year-old broke into uncontrollable sobs. The thirteen-year-old upon observing this, did a 180 degree turn-about, and told the officers everything. Based on her information, they obtained search warrants, and in one of the homes found photographs of 3 and 4-year-old boys and girls engaged in acts of sex, smoking cigarettes, and drinking beer. The thirteen-year-old was able to name all of these children, which, of course, resulted in more charges.

The runaway will seldom announce, "I ran away from home because my father was having sexual intercourse with me." She will more likely say "I can't get along with my father," or "They all hate me there." Patience is virtue.

# CHILDREN'S STORY

In exercising it, the officer should explore the family setting: brothers, sisters, aunts, or uncles in the home, grandparents, bedrooms, working hours, and so on. Finally, the officer should get to some ultimate question, "Is somebody bothering you at home?" In the universal language of children, "bothering" seems to be a very significant word. If someone is "bothering" the child at home, the initial reaction will often be silence. Officers should be trained to pursue the subject with quiet understanding. Investigators will get much more information by avoiding any suggestion of shock. The child already feels like a freak, as if she were the only one in the world this has ever happened to, and the first step for the officer is to convince her that the officer is not shocked. Probably the most effective approach is for the officer to indicate that the activity should stop. With a little common sense and compassion, the officer can show the child that not she, but Daddy, is the "freak."

Victims often want to know what will happen if they talk. The investigating officer should be prepared to answer those questions. A major concern of most victims at this juncture is "What is going to happen to my Dad?" The officer can honestly indicate that he or she doesn't know, those matters being left up to the courts. The officer should never lie to a child. The child's whole life has been rooted in lies. The criminal justice system should begin the healing process, not further victimize the child.

> During the investigation of a thoroughly horrible molestation case involving one man's three daughters—one 17, one 15, (both step-daughters), and an eleven-year-old natural daughter — the mother was so convincing in her ignorance that both the sheriff's deputy and the deputy district attorney allowed the three children to return home with her after incarcerating the man. She convinced both the deputy DA and the deputy sheriff of her ignorance of the situation, despite the fact that the seventeen-year-old had a child that looked just like step-daddy. Mother took the children home, bailed Daddy, and disappeared into the sunset, never to be seen again.

The other children in the family must be separately interviewed. Often the other children know what has been going on and, though reluctant, will share some information. Occasionally, siblings have walked into rooms while the molesting acts were taking place. That kind of corroboration clearly makes the case more than a one-on-one. It "ices it up." Defense counsel who will sincerely and passionately argue that a seven-year-old girl made everything up because she was jealous of her step-mother and wanted to get back at her, will be hard-pressed indeed to explain how she lured her five-year-old brother into this conspiracy to commit perjury. Appearing to the siblings to help the youngster in trouble is often the most successful approach for eliciting information. Even siblings who declare their hatred for each other will come to the defense of that child. The "hatred" often stems from the fact that the victim had been getting gifts or other special treatment as the price of her silence. Be on the alert. Are any other children in the home getting "special treatment?"

All of the children should have a medical examination. One child may be reporting the molest, but all the children in the family may be suffering. A medical examination, at least, insures that there is no physical injury. If a medical examination does reveal a venereal disease or injury to the genitals, follow up must be done.

### Informational Inquiry

Nearly all states now have reporting laws. Professionals in disciplines which deal with children are mandated to report suspected physical or sexual abuse. It is generally a misdemeanor not to report. There also may be civil liability connected with a failure to report and protection for people from civil liability who report in good faith. These statutes are also meant to encourage all people to participate in calling abuse of children to the attention of law enforcement agencies. Such calls may be made anonymously. The usual caller's preference is to remain anonymous, which can prove frustrating to law enforcement, but is probably ultimately advantageous in encouraging reports.

> I was just calling to ask what would happen if you knew that someone was messing around with his kid?" says the nervous and rushed voice on the other end of the phone.
>
> "Well, that would depend on what "messing around" was going on," replies the officer receiving the report.
>
> "You know, sexual stuff, and I mean it's like homo stuff," says the voice.
>
> "How old is the child?"
>
> "Ten."
>
> "How old is the man?"

# CHILDREN'S STORY

"In his thirties".

"Do you know what is going on between them sexually?"

"Well, yeah. I mean he's making the kid give him head."

"How did you find out about this?" "The kid told me. That's how I know." "Are you related in some way to this child?" "I'm not going to say. I just called to find out what would happen to the kid and the guy if you cops got on it." "Well, the first thing we would do would be to talk to the little boy ..."

"Yeah, yeah, I know all that. I want to know what you're going to do with the kid."

The caller has two primary concerns, 1) stopping abuse, and 2) making sure the kid isn't harmed by the system. The officer who take the call has no way of knowing which is the top priority concern. The evasiveness of the caller also indicates that he will be easily spooked. The officer should explain as much as he can. It should be made very clear that the child will not be placed with juvenile delinquents under any circumstances.

"The fact that you're calling indicates that you care very much about the welfare of this little boy. I wish I could tell you exactly what would happen, but I can't. I don't know enough at this point to tell you what would happen. You're probably concerned that I am going to come over there and grab him and he'll disappear into the system. I can't tell you at this point whether the young man would be taken into protective custody or not. I just don't have enough information. But I can tell you this. Your are quite right in your concern for him. He is in a very dangerous situation and we should put a stop to it."

Now, this is obviously a speech that is not going to come trippingly off the tongue. An officer will not have time to sit down and compose such an oration. The words must fit the situation, but the officer should:

1) acknowledge the caller's concern;

2) agree with the caller that there is good reason for concern;

3) recognize the caller's desire to stop the activity;

4) agree that the activity must stop;

5) demonstrate that he/she recognizes that the caller is fearful about the fate of the child;

6) speak truthfully about the fate of the child.

Credibility must be established at the beginning. The caller must be confident that the officer will be honest with him. After the officer has answered the initial questions, the caller has two choices, hang up the phone or tell you more about the case, including the child's identity. Even if the caller hangs up, the changes are excellent that he will call back once he has had an opportunity to mull the conversation over. But if he stays on the line and gives more information, the question of the caller's identity must be answered. Never go into this until after you have tried to get the victim's name. Protect the child first. Make a case later. If the caller is hesitant to reveal his name, the officer can assure him that he will do everything in his power to keep the caller's identity a secret, but should the case to go court, the caller might be asked to testify on behalf of the child. If the caller is willing to give his name or if he later calls back with the name, an interview and report should follow. The child's first discussion with the caller concerning his sexual abuse may be admissible under the "spontaneous statement" or "recent complaint" exception to the hearsay rule.

The caller will most often be an acquaintance of the molester. The officer cannot know and should not try to guess whether the caller wants the molester to get involved with the court system or not. If the caller is Daddy's next-door neighbor and bowling partner, you don't want to tell him that Daddy is going to prison. On the other hand, the caller may have no faith in the courts, and may hang up if he gets the impression that nothing is going to happen to this evil person, but he (caller) will get into a lot of trouble for blowing the whistle.

Informational inquires may also occur in person. The case discussed in Chapter 1 is typical. Grandmother appears at the front desk of the policing agency, eight-year-old granddaughter in tow When grandmother appears at the police station with the child, she will probably arrive expecting the police officer will take over, get to the bottom of the matter, make the child feel better, straight out the child's mother and castrate the offender, and do all this before the sun rises in the east. Grandmother must be separated from these notions.

The first problem the officer faces in this situation is calming Grandmother down. It is perfectly understandable that she is agitated and upset, but unbridled demonstrations of emotion serve only to convince the victim-child that her situation is desperate. The officer should spend some time with Grandmother, first listening to her, then assuring her that an investigation will take place, and finally that the best thing she can do for the child at this point is to calm down and support the child. Her demonstration of anger and sadness frightens the child. "The last thing in the world we want to do is have this little girl think that she is responsible for upsetting everyone. She might think she's a bad girl. And I know you don't want her to think that." After spending some time with Grandmother, the officer should turn his attention to the child. Officers handling these cases should not be in uniform. But uniformed or not, there are some interview techniques which can be used in any case to make the child more comfortable:

## Basic Interviewing Techniques

1) get out from behind the desk;

2) don't tower over the child;

3) sit close, but don't encroach on her territory;

4) spend a little time talking about other things;

5) tell her that Grandmother has already told you what happened;

6) let her tell the story in her own words; and
7) use a doll or pictures if that helps.

The initial interview is a great responsibility. The officer is looking for information, while endeavoring not to contaminate it. The process is made so much more difficult by the age of the victim. It requires a mixture of good police work, good interview techniques, sensitivity and some knowledge of child development.

Along with the interview techniques which aid the officer in gaining accurate information, there are "caution signs" which also should be noted. The vulnerability of children has made them into chameleons who will change color with the background. Some interviewers inadvertently pressure children to respond in certain ways. Children from dysfunctional homes often survive because they anticipate what an adult wants to see or hear. It serves no end of justice to report incorrect information.

The child has shared her secret with her grandmother, but the officer is her first involvement in the legal system. The system should seek to make it a favorable encounter. The child has a problem; the officer is here to "make it better." The technique most productive in getting information is to speak to the child one-one-one. Occasionally, however, a child simply will not talk without the presence of the reporting adult. Then, of course, the adult must remain.

One would hardly begin a conversation with an adult without exchanging a few pleasantries. Similarly, children should be accorded the same time and effort. The officer should talk about things which will interest the child, her pets, brothers, sisters, friends, and so on. Toys should be available for diversion. Officer and child should play for a while. The primary objective is to make the situation comfortable for the interviewer and the interviewed. The child is just waiting to hear the officer say, "So I'm told you're a queer."

It is difficult to know how to broach the subject of a child's molestation. One really doesn't want to begin with, "And so . . . when was the last time you were molested?" On the other hand, the officer cannot wait for the child to bring up the subject. One effective method of broaching the subject is telling the child that grandmother has already told of the events. Then the officer can repeat, with as much specificity as possible, what has been told. The officer then asks the child if that is what has happened to her. Once the victim has heard the words used by another, it is often much easier to engage in a discussion. Of course, there should be care taken not to put words in the mouth of the child.

In going over the facts with a child, she should be encouraged to use her own language and words in describing the incidents. Children don't ordinarily talk about penises and vaginas and acts of sexual intercourse and oral copulation. Children talk about "wieners" and "privates" and "jumping up and down on me" and "putting his pee pee in my mouth." She should be allowed the language which is most comfortable for her. Children's language is quite graphic and clear.

The use of dolls and/or pictures is sometimes helpful for shy children who are not very talkative. It is easier to point to an area of the body involved than to try to describe it in words. Anatomically correct dolls are available and prove a valuable asset to the policing agency.

At the end of the interview with the child-victim, the officer is left with the unfortunate task of deciding the child's immediate future. Does she go home? Does she go to the dependent children's home? Does she go with grandmother? If, during the interview, facts emerge which indicate that the

# CHILDREN'S STORY

mother had knowledge of the molest, or any abuse of the child, or if there is *anything* about the situation which makes the officer feel that the mother will be unable or unwilling to protect the child, the child should be booked in the dependent children's home. She cannot be sent home with the grandmother, because grandmother does not have legal custody. There would be nothing to prevent the mother or father from demanding the return of the child. Even if the child says that mother knew nothing, the mother must be interviewed before making an important decision to send the child home with her. If there are any doubts about the mother's stability, the agency should place the child in the dependent children's home. It is the job of the courts to decide on the eventual placement of the child.

# INVESTIGATION

# III.   EVALUATION AT INTAKE

*"...as a rule of thumb children should be taken seriously when allegations of sexual molestation are made."*

A "good" child molestation case is as rare as a hen's tooth. When a prosecutor evaluates a case at intake, no matter how brief that evaluation may be, a number of factors are being considered:

1. Is there, in fact, a crime?

2. What crime is it?

3. Is it, or are they, misdemeanors or felonies?

4. I.D.

5. What connects the defendant to the crime?

6. Is there a possibility of more evidence to come?

7. What defenses are available?

8. How strong is the witness' testimony?

In the following sections, these eight factors will be considered one by one. The ideal methods of evaluating a child molestation case is to interview the child before issuing the complaint. Interview is not always possible. Usually, the evaluation will be done on the basis of police reports. Therefore, it is clearly preferable that the reports be prepared by well trained and articulate officers. If prosecutors and officers are trained to handle these cases together, reports should give the prosecutor, at intake, a clear picture and feeling for the case.

The case at hand is the eight-year-old girl brought in by her grandmother.

### 1) Is there, in fact, a crime?

The little girl says that her "generic Daddy" (be it father, step-father, Mommy's live-in boyfriend, or some other father figure) has fondled her over the past six months and that she has orally copulated him and he has orally copulated her. Although the police report doesn't specify how many times this actually happened, or how many individual acts can be designated, there are at least three crimes.

## 2) What crime is it?

Each separate and distinct incident can give rise to a separate charge. The only limitation is the ability of the prosecution to pinpoint distinct incidents. Overcharging is seldom advantageous. There is little time, generally, for a great deal of preparation and the available time is better spent making the child comfortable with a discussion of the events which stand out most clearly in her mind. If the preliminary hearing reveals additional specific, but uncharged counts, these counts can be filed on the information. Charging zeal should be tempered by the knowledge that eventually there must be a disposition case. No matter what the in any given jurisdiction, it simply does not look good for a party connected with the case to have multiple felonies dismissed. The prosecutor is bound to the charges on the information. It would be unfair to expect an eight-year-old to be responsible for keeping multiple incidents at instant recall.

## 3) Is it, or are they, misdemeanors or felonies?

There is no calculus whereby a prosecutor can determine the character of the charges. Many crimes can be prosecuted both as misdemeanors and a felony. Misdemeanors and felonies meet in the grey area. Someone who lurks outside of a school, leering at children as they walk home, or says dirty words to children while lurking about has strayed over the line from the merely inappropriate to the misdemeanor area. In contrast, someone who ties a child, beats, chokes and forcefully penetrates a child has guaranteed a felony prosecution. The more difficult cases for everyone involved are those in which the child has been subjected to substantial sexual conduct, but no force of penetration have occurred.

These cases are often as destructive to the child as a more forceful experience, depending, of course, on all the circumstances. Each of these crimes must be analyzed individually. Consider Mommy's live-in boyfriend who grabs the breasts of Mommy's 13-year-old daughter. Technically, this is a felony conduct, but justice may be more appropriately served by granting a misdemeanor probation which would include daily A.A. meetings, group counseling, stay away orders and some appropriate amount of jail time.

Then there is the old neighborhood lecher who is bordering on senility. This man is the kindly grandfather of the neighborhood who lures the children into the garage with candy and gum for his own nefarious purposes. There he fondles the genitals of the children. His wife and grown children, upon hearing of the activities, immediately make arrangements to move him to a retirement village where no children are allowed. They swear that they will keep a tight rein on him. Now this man has also committed a felony, and depending upon his history, perhaps, that is how the case should be prosecuted. But, it might also be a candidate for a less vigorous prosecution.

Of course, there are many variations of these themes. If the prosecutor is in a quandary as to the proper charge, it may be best to err of the side of the felony. The preliminary hearing will often provide a much better perspective of the case. After the hearing, if the misdemeanor is the more appropriate charge, it can be filed in municipal court. The felony charge should be filed if the facts elicited indicate a problem which is deep seated, pervasive and likely to occur again. The longer probationary period available in felonies may be a more desirable result, even if state prison does not seem realistic or desirable.

## 4) Identification?

The most insignificant problem related to most child molestation cases is the identification. Almost without exception, the child molester is someone close to the child. It seems only fair that there be one easy part to this puzzle.

If the child is too small to testify, there are cases in which a fresh complaint can be combined with physical evidence. If the fresh complaint relates to physical evidence, the case should be triable. For example, if Robby (age 3) tells his mother, upon returning from his uncle's home, that his "Uncle Ed stuck his peter in my butt," and a physical examination reveals bruising and tearing of the rectal tissue, the evidence should be sufficient, even though Robby is too inarticulate to testify. An older child, competent to testify, may have observed the acts performed upon a younger child, not competent to testify. That older child's testimony alone may be enough for prosecution.

Occasionally physical evidence combined with a totally inadequate explanation of the injury by the suspect will be sufficient to establish the identity of the perpetrator.

A seventeen-month-old baby exhibiting a prolapsed rectum with bruising and tearing of the surrounding tissue and abraded skin in a circular pattern around the anus is admitted to the hospital. The gynecologist and pediatrician are competent to testify that an object at least 2" in diameter was forced into the anus. They will also testify that the abraded area is a result of something or someone rubbing the skin vigorously. They are further prepared to testify that the injuries are consistent with adult penis penetration. The suspect father, after proper *Miranda*, informs the investigating officer that the injures are the result of the child swallowing a piece of glass and subsequently passing that piece of glass. A call back to the doctor indicates that the majority of the tears are at the opening of the anus and that none exist up inside the colon. The doctor's opinion is that this is a clear indication that something has been forced in from the outside. When confronted with this information, the father suddenly remembers that he tried to get the glass out with a spoon. Bingo! As a prosecutor you've just been handed a dream come true. Either he is guilty of sodomizing his child, or he is guilty of felony child abuse, or both. Just imagine yourself saying on cross-examination, "And isn't it true, Mr. Jones, that you have a Medi-Cal card for little Janie? Why then did you not take her to the hospital? That must really have hurt, did she bleed?" The possibilities of cross-examination would be limited only by the prosecutor's creativity.

### 5) What connects the defendant to the crime?

Access to the child is the first indicator. Police should be trained to routinely ask questions to ascertain access to the child. The child says that "Daddy" (children use the term loosely to mean Mommy's present partner) did strange things to her. These things would happen when Mommy went to work. The investigation reveals that Mommy does work and "Daddy" is the babysitter. He even admits to that role, though denying any sexual activity.

Rarely is there physical evidence to corroborate the child's statements:

physical trauma, sexually transmitted infections, sperm, panties with semen on them. If such evidence is available, it should be treated as such evidence would be treated in a rape case. That is, it should be sent to the lab for forensic work-up. All the appropriate samples should be obtained from Mommy and Daddy, either by consent or through a court order, for comparison.

Very, very rarely a case will appear where someone actually viewed the crime. Cases have arisen in which relatives have arrived unexpectedly and found the acts in progress. A prosecutor could grow old waiting for a case with that type of evidence.

## 6) Possibility of more evidence to come.

The investigating agency should always talk to the defendant. The officer may have felt the case was so strong that he didn't want to give the suspect an opportunity to lie about it. The known is always preferable to the unknown. The case should be sent for further investigation. On rare occasions, the defendant may actually confess to the act or acts. Such a confession and demonstrated remorse indicate that the prosecutor and courts might look to a treatment program. If the statement is going to take a day or so, the issuing of the case should be held in abeyance, assuming, of course, that the child is in a safe place. Waiting until the statement is taken before filing the complaint recognizes that many officers lose interest in the case and feel their involvement ends at filing.

If the medical evidence isn't available because the parents or custodians of the child refuse to sign medical releases, then the case must be filed in order to obtain subpoena duces tecum.

The longer the child is away from the threat of molestation, the more information she will give. The longer "Daddy" remains in the home, the more convinced she will become that she is the offender. Filing the complaint and arresting the "Daddy" may help her believe that the molestation will stop. The child will consequently be more comfortable in giving further information.

## 7) What defenses are available to a defendant in a child molestation case?

In evaluating a case for prosecution, it is always reassuring to have some idea of the defense. Obviously, there will be times when no one knows the nature of the defense. The standard defenses are generally one of the following: absolute denial, some other dude done it, the child is fantasizing, the child is lying, the child and the world have misinterpreted his intentions, these allegations are the result of a messy dissolution of marriage and the mother is programming the child to say these things, the child was coached by a therapist with an overactive imagination.

All cases ultimately turn on the credibility of the witnesses. Molestation cases are no exception. If the prosecution witnesses are truthful, the prosecutors job becomes one of preparing those witnesses for the experience of court. The difficulty there lies in the fact that the complaining witness is disadvantaged by reason of age. Therefore, more time and more effort goes into the preparation. False allegations, though infrequent, are a reality. The prosecutor, policing agencies, and other services must acknowledge this reality. The time has passed when the simplistic, "Children don't lie," summed up the situation. In the early evolution of child sexual molestation prosecution, that sentence served the letting professionals know that they should not put on a Freudian mantle of doubt when faced with disclosures. Evolution and public acknowledgement of the problem, along with media coverage has resulted in an upswing in false allegations.

This is not to suggest that once again all disclosures should be viewed with a jaundiced eye. What it means, is that professionals at all levels must be better trained and more willing to look at each case critically. Dissolution may, in rare cases, result in an allegation of sexual molestation being made. It may be that neither the mother or the father are acting maliciously. It may be that the emotional upheaval occasioned by the split has cast innocent acts in a suspicious light.

> The father of these children had been isolated from both the mother of his children and his children during the 10 years of marriage. He never assumed any child care role, and he spent no time in play with the children. Upon dissolution of the marriage, he began to regret the lack of a relationship with his children. He determined to make up for his previous deficiency by taking the children places, spending time with them, playing games with them and touching them.
>
> The mother, already confused and upset, interpreted such behavior as abnormal and sexual in motivation. Each time the children returned they were questioned at length about how

game, the mother was convinced that the touching was fondling. A report was made to the policing agency.

This was not a case of anyone lying or intentionally trying to gain an advantage, it was a case where the facts as stated were true, but the conclusion was wrong. While such a scenario could properly be handled in a family law court, it has no place in the criminal justice system.

There may also be occasions where under-trained therapists may leap to conclusions which are unfounded, but there is no evidence that therapists program children to claim molestation. In fact, quite the contrary, under-trained therapist often overlook common indicators of molestation in dealing with troubled children and their families.

As a rule of thumb, children should be taken seriously when allegations of sexual molestation are made. But a simplistic approach which does not admit to examination does not serve the interest of society, the defendant or the child.

## 8) How strong is the child's testimony?

The majority of children from 6 to 12 years old are smart enough to record information, articulate enough to share it, and innocent enough to lack the skill of lying.

A case which presents a child under the age of 6, where corroboration is absent, is a case where the ability of the child to testify is the deciding factor. That factor cannot be decided until the prosecutor has an opportunity to talk to the child. Children as young as 3 can be competent to testify, but the child must be able to understand the questions and articulate an answer. In order to qualify as a witness, you must show that the child understands her obligation to tell the truth and know that some earthly consequence can befall him/her for lying. This is not to suggest, however, that the child must be incredibly bright. A normal child, under 6, with good verbal skills, is often a competent and a wildly successful witness, even though the child may tend to digress upon occasion. Question: "And did it hurt when he put his 'thing' between your legs?"

Answer: "Yes, that hurt, but not as much as when Debbie pinched me right here. See where she pinched me? She was mad 'cause I wouldn't go outside and play with Igor."

Such spontaneity should be welcomed. The child's inherent credibility lies in just such spontaneity. The child witness, ideally, should not appear rigid and rehearsed.

A child-victim or witness older than 12 doesn't have the same built-in credibility of a younger child. With an older child, there is more of a likelihood that the jury will be willing to entertain an argument that the child is making up the story to punish the defendant for some real or imagined wrong. Although, the old child generally has greater verbal skills, she has a proportionately greater share of guilt and embarrassment. Any indication in the crime report that the older child is reluctant to discuss the matter should result in an early interview with the child. The problem with the old child is generally making the child feel comfortable, with the prosecutor and with the subject.

# IV.   BEFORE TRIAL

*"...if nothing else is accomplished the child must be helped to believe that it is not her fault."*

There are a few simple and sensible techniques that can help the prosecutor prepare a child molestation victim for court. No child witness should be sent into court without being made ready to go one-on-one with her molester:

1. Meeting the child;

2. Discussing feelings;

3. Discussing the case;

4. Outrageous behavior;

5. Playing courtroom;

6. The day of testimony;

7. After the preliminary hearing.

## Meeting the Child

Arrange to meet the child prior to the date of testimony. More than in any other kind of case, it is imperative that child molesters be *vertically, prosecuted*. A feeling of trust and confidence between the prosecutor and the victim is crucial to the case. If this rapport is not established, the case will never get off the ground.

Whenever possible, the initial meeting between the prosecutor and the victim should take place at the present residence of the child. Prosecutors like to stay in their offices and have witnesses come to them, and in most cases, a busy schedule justifies doing so. In the case of a child, however, a feeling of security and trust should be built in the child at the outset. The child's security has never been too firm and recently has been totally destroyed. If meeting her at home is completely impossible, then she should be made as comfortable as possible in the D.A.'s surroundings. Offices should be set up to delight children. The walls should be covered with bright and cheerful pictures. Crayons and other toys should be made available. The attorneys should encourage the receptionists to greet the child with warmth and friendliness.

After the child has been greeted with a smile and pleasantries, the prosecutor should introduce herself and explain the purpose of the meeting. The facts of the case should not be the first subject of conversation. Speak to the child as you would to a new acquaintance. Brusque professionalism is out of place because the child does not know how to deal with it. The talk should center on things that are interesting to the child. School, ice cream, candy, puppies, kittens, brothers and sisters are quick possibilities. Let the child be the guide. Since children thrive on physical activity, show and tell is frequently a good place to start. She can be shown the office, allowed to photograph her hands at the Xerox machine, and introduced to other people around the office. A prosecutor with a natural rapport with kids obviously has an advantage, but almost anyone can develop the needed skills.

The attorney must appear relaxed, friendly, and at ease. Children are much more attuned to physical signals than verbal ones. Child victims are frequently described as being watchful or vigilant. They have had to learn to read adults by physical messages, and to distrust verbal ones. The child-victim is told by her abuser that she is loved and that she is special, but the brutal physical reality communicates dominance and lack of concern. People who deal with such a child, including the prosecutor, must be sensitive to non-verbal communication. The watchful and vigilant child may begin to relax upon seeing the attorney put his feet up on the desk or sitting on the floor. The necessity of establishing a relaxed and friendly atmosphere does not allow the traditional professional approach.

Touching is very important. No matter how seemingly insignificant, touching gives the person touched a feeling of warmth. But a child who has been used and abused by an adult may not at first welcome overt displays of affection. The touching suggested for this first meeting is merely the slightest touching of her hand or her face. Then again, some children overwhelm everyone around them with their need for physical closeness. This need should be accepted, but the child must also learn that she cannot constantly force her attentions on others. Sensitive adults will establish limits. None of these children are hot-house plants. They are survivors and consequently can take criticism and accept limits. Loving firmness is the ideal environment for both the child and the prosecutor. These children need to learn that touching need not be sexual or manipulative, but only warm, loving and safe.

## Discussing Feelings

Once the child has learned that all adults are not ogres, the time is right to enter into a discussion about feelings. If the child is out of the home, ask her how she feels about it. Adults often jump to the hasty conclusion that the child is going to be happy as a clam about being free of the threat of molestation. Such a reaction is actually quite rare. The child should be encouraged to express her feelings — good, bad, or angry. There is no judgment to be passed on her feelings no matter what they are.

It is even more important to ascertain the victim's feelings towards the defendant. Do not assume that the child hates the molester. He is often the only man in her life. She has no basis for comparison. As discussed previously, the child has, in many cases, been paid off in one way or another for her favors. Those feelings can then be reflected back to her. "I'll bet he was really nice to you lots of the time. You love him and he loves you, but he did some things to you that he really shouldn't have done." With this approach, the child learns that her feelings are O.K., that she is understood, that the problem lies in the acts and not in the feelings, and that someone cares and is on her side. It is sometimes wrong to act on feelings, but in themselves, feelings are never wrong.

Prosecutors should avoid picturing themselves as avenging angels swooping down to set right the lives of these children. Frequently, the prosecutor will be viewed by the child as the betrayer — part of the system which has torn her world apart. She has told her story in a moment of desperation, never imagining the far-reaching consequences. Though she wanted the activity to stop, she did not want to be taken to a detention facility. She did not want the man to go to a prison. She did not want her mother mad at her. A prosecutor troubled by the intensity of the child's feelings should remind herself that young children cannot make major decisions about their lives. Children are ruled by the immediacy of the moment, which is, of course, what makes them such easy targets.

Guilt and shame are feelings that young children harbor, but have no way of expressing. Older victims often acknowledge such feelings. One exercise for dealing with these feelings is fun and silly, and brings home an incredibly important message. The attorney says, "Now, none of this is your fault. Little kids can't help what big people do to them. Kids don't have very many ways to say no." The child should then be asked to say, "It's not my fault." The first time she will probably whisper the line. The attorney says, "I can't hear you! You're going to have to say that a little louder." As the attorney backs away from her, across the room or across the hall, the child is asked to say it louder and louder, until finally she is yelling it. Kids like to yell, and if the attorney relaxes and perhaps even yells too, this can be a good therapeutic sport for both players.

If nothing else is accomplished, the child must be helped to believe that it is *not* her fault.

Ascertaining a child's feelings towards the offender also enables the prosecutor to decide which path to take in explaining the judicial process to the child. Obviously a prosecutor would take differing approaches depending on whether the child still loves the offender and is feeling guilty about "telling on Daddy" or truly feels victimized and hates the offender.

In the first case, the best approach is to explain that, "Daddy has a problem." Give the child the satisfaction of arriving at the conclusion that she is helping Daddy by testifying. For example:

Question: Do you think what your Daddy did was right?

Answer: (Child will invariably answer — NO!)

Question: Would you want your Daddy to do that to someone else? (Personalize question by inserting names of siblings if there are any.)

Question: Your Daddy has a problem, doesn't he?

Answer: (Again, child will inevitably answer — YES.)

Question: Do you know you can help your Daddy with his problem?

Answer: How?

Prosecutor: By telling the judge what his problem is. That's what judges are for. We go to them when we have a problem that we need their help with. But before the judge can know what kind of help your daddy needs, he has to know what kind of problem your daddy has.

Its just like going to a doctor. A doctor can't know how to help you until he knows how you hurt. But sometimes even dads aren't brave enough to admit their problems and that's why your dad needs your help in explaining his problem.

If, on the other hand, a child is scared of and/or dislikes the offender, a helpful approach is as follows: DDA: Are you thinking you're going to be embarrassed to tell the judge what Moe (molester) did?

# CHILDREN'S STORY

Child: Yeah...
DDA: Well you know what?
Child: What?
DDA: The judge has heard these kinds of things before. He's heard from lots of other kids who have had the same problems you have had and even worse. (*Children need* to be constantly reminded that they are not the only ones in the world who have been similarly victimized. To bring this point home, prosecutors who specialize in such cases can point to all the other case files in their office and explain that these are cases that you have right now where kids just like them were molested and are going to court too.) But the judge doesn't think you're bad and you shouldn't be embarrassed. But you know who *will* be embarrassed?
Child: Who?
DDA: Moe. Because he has to just sit there and listen and NOT SAY A WORD while you tell the judge what HE DID. The judge is just going to be sad that these things happened to you. He's not going to think you're bad. You know who he *will* think is bad, don't you?
Child: (As a light goes on in her head...) Moe!! As a prosecutor, just watch your child-victim sit a little straighter in her chair and feel better about herself and the system. For many children, far from being damaging, testifying against their molester can actually be beneficial because it teaches them many much needed lessons, e.g., no one thinks they're bad or responsible for the molestation and adults will listen and believe them when they tell what they've been subjected to.

## Discussing the Case

Now is the time to turn the discussion to the facts of the case. "Now I'm going to tell you what I think happened with you and John. If I make any mistakes, you tell me I'm wrong." The story is then told using the child's own words for body parts and physical acts, which should be contained in the crime report. Be as specific as possible. Specificity accomplishes two things. First, the child learns that you already know the story. Secondly, the prosecutor has said those nasty words first. As the story is recounted, the attorney can stop occasionally, falter and get confused, and ask the child to straighten out the sequence of events. If not too many questions are asked, she will generally be willing to help out in putting the scenario together.

The prosecutor, having gone through the story once, now turns to the victim to have her tell the story in her own words. At this point, the pro-secutor's part should be, "What happened next? Then what did he do? Where were you? Where was your mom? Where was the dog?"

Children love to tell stories and it is difficult, if not impossible, to lead them. The child should be encouraged to tell about the events in her own way and in her own words. Certain words may be difficult for her to say. Certain acts may be difficult for her to describe. The attorney who fills in the words or describes the acts with a complete lack of embarrassment will convince the child that it really is OK to in the courtroom. The prosecutor should start moving farther and farther away, explaining that she is going to have to speak loudly and clearly.

Specific incidents are the most important part of the case. The child must be able to describe the events that are the basis of the complaint. Dates, though obviously helpful, needn't concern anyone a great deal at this point. Most children can't give them. This information can sometimes be deduced from other occasions in the child's life — Christmas, her birthday, Hallo-ween, where she was living at that time, or what grade she was in. Calen-dar dates are not imperative so long as the occasions are clear and distinct. Molestations are usually alleged to have occurred between certain dates. As long as the child can relate specific occurrences within a framework of these dates, the burden of specificity has been met. It is often possible to subpoena adults to give more accurate information as to dates. The inter-view should not be cluttered with side issues. The child is the lead actress in this case, and her stage should not be flooded with insignificant details.

### Outrageous Behavior on the Part of the Prosecutor

Some children will crumple like a wet paper bag when the details of the case are mentioned.

> One little girl buried her face in the shoulder of the sheriff's deputy whenever the case was mentioned. She indicated that she would talk to the prosecutor about any number of things as long as it didn't involve the man or the events which had brought her to the prosecutor's office.
>
> She listened with one eye fixed on the prosecutor as he recounted the story. She would nod her head when asked if cer-tain things had happened to her. She finally agreed, after having been wrestled from the lap of the deputy, to answer yes or no,

but would not say those awful words or describe those awful events herself. Undaunted, the prosecutor reached for the last trick in the bag — the Outrageous. As he recounted the story of the child's oral copulation of the adult, a mischievous look appeared on his face. "Did stuff come out of the end of his pee pee?" She nodded, now fascinated by the smile. The prosecutor pressed on, "Did it go in your mouth?" She nodded again, still watching the smile which was getting broader. "Did it come out of your ears?" The prosecutor giggled and the little girl couldn't help giggling also. "Did it come out between your toes?" Through the giggles she managed to say, "No, no!" The prosecutor, making a terrible face, asked, "How did it taste?" The girl yelled, "Yukky!" Voila! The ice was broken. The prosecutor said, "I'll bet it was yukky." She said, "Yeah, and he wouldn't even let me spit it out. I had to swallow it." The prosecutor responded, "That must have made you feel like you wanted to throw up." The girl agreed, and the conversation continued from there.

A child must be dealt with on her own level. These victims are not cosmopolitan adults who have a sense of good taste and propriety. They are children, accustomed to relating to events like children. Continuing to ask pat questions to which the only response is a frozen stare is a fruitless and frustrating experience for both prosecutor and child. In the above example, the prosecutor managed to communicate in child's language, catch the child's attention, and share a silly joke. At the same time, as the child began to talk, the prosecutor was reflecting her feelings back to her and validating those feelings.

Often others will be in the room as the interviewer progresses. Children need to be shown that adults won't mind hearing these words. It is a good idea to have both men and women present, to help the child get over the discomfort of breaking the taboo of using these words in public.

In one instance in which a child simply couldn't get out the words, "He put his pee pee in my mouth," the prosecutor had already told the story with which the little girl agreed. When she was asked to begin telling the story, she did a fine job until she got to that phrase. At that point, she would redden, hang her head, and say, "I can't say that." The prosecutor asked her if the defendant had, in fact, done that thing to her. She would nod.

The prosecutor then turned to the sheriff's officer who happened to be in the room, and said, "You say, 'he put his pee pee in my mouth.'" "The officer said, "He put his pee pee in my mouth." Turning to the worker from the Child Protective Services, the prosecutor asked her to do the same. The worker got very nervous, cleared her throat, and after a couple of shaky starts managed to croak out the sentence, looking agonizingly uncomfortable the whole time. The officer and the prosecutor laughed.

The worker started to laugh, realizing how tough those words are to get out. Soon the child started to laugh and the prosecutor turned to her and said, "Say, 'He put his pee pee in my mouth.'" Still giggling, the little girl pointed to the social worker and said, "He put his pee pee in her mouth." The shared joke relaxed the atmosphere and the child was eventually able to say those words in court.

Magical thinking leads children to believe that they are the center of the universe. Almost without exception, they think they are the first and the only person to have experienced such behavior with an adult. It is important for them to know that these acts have been practiced upon many other children. One prosecutor kept drawings and gifts from other various child witnesses and would show them to new witnesses, indicating that they were from other kids who had been in the same boat. The new witnesses frequently will want more information about what happened to these other children. Answer the questions, but keep the answers brief.

For the occasional child who remains mute no matter what, engaging in some physical activity may break the barrier. Often children who will not talk will draw pictures. Prosecutor and child can sit on the floor and draw pictures. Eventually they can begin to discuss the drawings and eventually move on. It may be necessary to take a walk or play with dolls. The fact that the prosecutor is willing to change gears and communicate on the child's level often will give the child the confidence to open up.

The foregoing suggestions and examples are just that—suggestions and examples. Each prosecutor must develop his or her own style. Interest and humor are a great aid in dealing with all witnesses, but these qualities are even more important when dealing with children who must be helped over the hurdles of communicating persuasively about the kind of secret that no one, not even the most mature adult is eager to share with others.

# CHILDREN'S STORY

## Playing Courtroom

Prior to the day of testimony, it is important to play court. If possible, the child should be taken to the courtroom and introduced to the clerk, the bailiff, and the judge. Needless to say, the facts of the case will not be discussed. But intro,duction will let her know that the awesome person in the black robe and the clerk who rattles off the witness's oath are just nice, ordinary people. Go into the courtroom and play a game of "where does everyone sit?" Have the clerk swear the child in the witness's chair, then ask her if she understands what she has just promised to do. Nine times out of ten, the answer will be, "no." She should be told that she has just promised to tell the truth. "Do you know what it means to tell the truth?" The answer will probably be "yes." Then the question, "What is the truth?" should be asked. Her response will generally be, "I don't know." The prosecutor then says, "The truth is what really happened. If I told you that I just went to the moon for lunch, would that be what really happened? No, that is not the truth. If it told you that my face is blue with pink polka dots, is that the truth or a lie?" She says, "That's a lie." A few more questions along this line will establish that the child does, indeed, know the difference between the truth and a lie. Since one of the favorite questions of defense attorneys is "Have you ever told a lie?" the prosecutor may want to deal with this point now. Prosecutor: Have you ever told a lie?
Child: Yes Prosecutor: Have you ever been caught telling a lie?
Child: Yes. Prosecutor: What happened?
Child: I got spanked.

or—

Prosecutor: Have you ever told a lie?
Child: No.
Prosecutor: I have.
Child: I haven't.
Prosecutor: I bet you have. Has your mother ever punished you for telling
        a lie?
Child: Sometimes.
Prosecutor: How does she punish you?
Child: She makes me stand in the corner.
Prosecutor: Then you have told a lie.
Child: Not very often.

51

While the child is in the witness box, the prosecutor should sit in the appropriate seat and make sure the conversation is loud enough for all parties to hear. Every person has a place in the courtroom, the clerk, the judge, the court reporter, the bailiff, the defense attorney and the defendant. If she knows this ahead of time, and knows where everyone will be and what their respective responsibilities are, the day of the actual testimony will not be so frightening.

Unless identity of the defendant is a central issue, it is important for the child to know that the offender will be in the courtroom. She must be told that he is going to be there when she tell what he did to her. She must also be told that she will have to point him out as the man who did these things to her. Not to tell her this would be tantamount to telling a child that a spinal tap won't hurt. While it is important to play and have fun, it is equally important to be honest about the unpleasantries involved. Upon hearing that the offender will be present, some children tell everyone that they cannot go through with it. By explaining to the child that nothing bad can happen to her in the courtroom, some of these fears will be alleviated. Stress the fact that a bailiff or officer will be in the court at all times and he is on her side and will make sure the molester doesn't do anything, but sit quietly in his chair. When the time comes to testify, the prosecutor can do all manner of things to keep the child's attention focused. Standing up, moving around, sitting down, getting her water, rattling papers, and keeping eye contact with her are all ways to make the courtroom disappear.

The child should be informed that someone besides the prosecutor is going to ask her questions — the defense attorney. "This other guy who is going to sit right here is going to ask you some questions, too. You don't have to look at him, you can still look at me. But listen to the questions and answer them with the truth. Just tell the truth and everything will be OK. Do you have any questions that you want to ask me?" The prosecutor must be most persuasive at this time. "You don't have to look at him. You just keep on looking at me." If the defense attorney is known to have any favorite questions or particular courtroom habits, tell them to the child. On the other hand, if the attorney is known to be easy on child witnesses, the prosecutor might consider introducing the child to him a few days before court. A few things will damage a defense attorney's mental preparation for cross examination as much as the grim realization, that the victim is telling the truth, is ready to testify, and will be able to do so effectively. Child victims are almost always secreted by the family or the prosecution, but this is not always wise.

## The Day of Testimony

Assuming that prosecutor and child have had an opportunity to meet and discover the events in question, the day of the preliminary hearing is no time to go over testimony. This is a time for discussing feelings about what she is about to do, how pretty she looks, how glad everyone will be when this is over, and so on. Once again, the child should be reassured that it is not her fault, even though it may seem that she's the one who is being punished.

Children are just small witnesses. Witnesses react in different fashions to the experience of testifying. Some are eager, some fall apart, and some just want to get it over with. The same is true of children. Since they tend to mirror the demeanor of adults, the prosecutor should exude confidence. The child should walk without support to the courtroom. She should stand up straight and not collapse on the prosecutor or on anyone else. Allowing her to clutch and cling imparts a message to her that there must be something really scary coming up. Instead, she should play Super-Girl. Assuring her of how tough she is and how she's going to go in and take care of business has the effect of a self-fulfilling prophecy.

Then comes the oath and the actual testimony. Often tears will form and chins will quiver. Attorneys should not stop at the first sign of crying. If the child sees the person in front of her continuing to smile and showing of confidence, she will begin to mirror that relaxed attitude provided the proper relationship has been established.

Direct examination should consists most of, "What happened next?" This gives the witness an opportunity to tell the story in her own words. Details are not necessary. The only requirement is that each element of the crime be described, and that each incident be specific.

After direct examination, the prosecutor has the pleasure of watching the defense attorney try to deal with the child. Here are some snappy examples of devastating cross-examination of child molest victims:

Defense Attorney to eight-year-old: You hate your daddy, don't you?

Eight-year-old: No, I love my daddy. Defense Attorney: You're mad at your daddy. Eight-year-old: Only when he makes me suck his dick.

Defense Attorney: How big was his pee pee?

Child: (indicates four inches)

Defense Attorney: (turns to judge and asks) Could the record reflect that the child has indicated approximately four inches?

Child: (interjects before the judge can reply) Yeah, but after he made me suck on it for a while, it was this big. (child indicates about eight inches)

Defense Attorney: Your Honor, I would ask that the court strike that last statement. There was no question asked of the witness.

Defense Attorney to an exceptionally bright 11-year-old boy who had been repeatedly sodomized by his father: How long has this been going on?

11-year-old: I suppose in most families this would be unusual. Unfortunately, in mine, it was quite usual.

Most defense attorneys are ill-prepared to deal with a child witness. The most common defense mistake is assuming that the child can be led down the primrose path. Young children simply know what has happened and are not clever enough to anticipate the answers that people are looking for. If the child does get into any problems on cross-examination, those problems can be cleared up on redirect when, once again, the child is allowed to tell the story in her own words.

As increasing numbers of these cases hit the courts, increased sophistication in the defense has occurred. The defense may seek to show that the child is not capable of answering some questions. What happens is the defense attorneys and sometimes the trier-of-fact confuse sophistication with credibility and competence. The prosecutor must be sure that the trier-of-fact, whether judge or jury understands that language skills should and must not be confused with ability to tell the truth. They must be educated to the fact that the child can answer questions within his or her linguistic competence. For instance, it is absurd to think that a five-year-old child is capable of responding to compound, complex questions. A simple rule of thumb is that children of tender years are capable of understanding statements with words which number no more than the number of years in the child's age plus one. In the case of the aforementioned five-year-old, a six word question.

The defense attorney who attempts to badger and bully the child must be stopped with objections of badgering and argumentative. Most judges will not allow a child to be abused. If screaming and yelling are necessary to divert the defense attorney's attention from the child, the prosecutor must scream and yell. The child has already been victimized and cannot be subjected to further victimization. If possible, a recess should be taken to assure the child that this anger is not directed to her. An angry or hostile environment is presumed by children to be directly their fault. A child witness can be warned that this is just the way the lawyers act, and that it really has nothing to do with her. Many children will attempt to avoid answering questions by diverting their own attention. Some will swivel back and forth in the chair with such monotonous regularity that those watching feel that they are at a ping pong match. Some will carefully shred a tissue. Others will twist a piece of hair. These mindless repetitions are a child's way of avoid the task at hand. The conduct has to be stopped. "Ellen, look at me. Sit up straight. Put your hands in your lap." It may be necessary for the judge or attorney to remove the diversion, or take her hands and put them in her lap. The child's attention is a necessity.

The child has been encouraged to stand on her own two feet and maintain a strong demeanor prior to and during the preliminary hearing. Now, after the hearing, she should get a great deal of praise and support. She should be allowed to fall apart, be angry, be sad or express whatever other emotion she deems appropriate. Upon her departure she should once again be reminded, "This is not your fault. Do you know that?"

## After the Preliminary Hearing

Once the defendant is held to answer, the child will probably disappear from the prosecutor's life for a while, maybe forever. Saying goodbye will generally be a mixture of relief and sadness relief that the child has been given a voice, relief that the child has been given support, and emotional involvement, relief that she may go on living with less guilt and with more sensible feelings of anger and outrage. However, one can hardly avoid the sadness of knowing that this child is being sent to an unknown future with little, if any, support.

It is important to mention that many molested children are not adorable, not even likeable. Many of them are angry, aggressive, and generally obnoxious little brats. They are difficult, if not impossible, to love. Although loving or even deeply liking such children may be impossible, understanding the process that made them unlovable should make dealing with them easier.

The final act, for the former victim is frequently suicide. Some of these suicides are apparent and some are written off as drug-related deaths or accidents. These results suggest that the solution for many female molestation victims is self-destruction.

While the girls are busily destroying themselves and those closest to them, male molestation victims tend to externalize their anger, lashing out violently at others. Understanding the damage done in childhood to these young men does not make them any less dangerous, nor does it excuse their behavior, but it does point out that early and effective intervention is really the only hope for breaking the pattern of violence. Both male and female molestation victims need radical intervention and extensive counseling, both for themselves and for their families.

Most counties offer services to families and children caught up in this cycle. If your county offers such services, familiarize yourself with them, and encourage participation by all family members. Your brief encounter with the child, your support, and your approval are important, but ongoing therapy is always indicated. Prisons warehouse dangerous people for a short period of time, but the myth of rehabilitation was relinquished years ago. The sins of the parents are visited upon the sons and daughters.

# V.    JURY TRIAL

*"...you are going to tell what happened and those twelve people are going to know you are telling the truth."*

If a preliminary hearing fails to produce a guilty plea from the defendant, the jury trial should be calendared as soon as possible. Time works amazing changes on people's memories and the child-victim is not exception. Time dulls memory, and children actively try to forget unpleasant experiences. There is a growing body of evidence that also shows that the longer the child is in contact with "the system," the greater are the possibilities that the child will end up engaging in some form of delinquent activity. It seems that if the child does not have a quick and effective adjudication, he loses respect for the system. This information alone should encourage a speedy and effective intervention and an equally speedy and effective withdrawal.

Some children will remain in the home. Some will be in foster homes; some with relatives. Many have the support of family members; others must go it alone. Some receive effective therapy most do not. And so it goes. But the passage of time has one constant result in all situations. The longer the delay between the initial report and the final disposition, the more likely it is that the family will attempt to back out of prosecution. Anger subsides; embarrassment grows (along with the financial and family problems.)

Upon her return to the courthouse, the child should be greeted with warmth and affection. The confidence and concern imparted to her early on will bear fruit now. With luck, there will be an opportunity to sit down with the child and chat with her before the day of the trial. This is an opportunity to re-establish the child's security; the approach employed before the preliminary hearing is equally good here, and you will find the relationship of trust and confidence easier to establish this time.

Before the day of the trial, the prosecutor, victim, and other interested parties should visit the empty courtroom to reacquaint the child with the mechanics of courtroom procedure. Although the courtroom is a familiar place to the prosecutor, it is a brief view of purgatory to the twelve people who will occupy it. "Twelve people are going to sit here and listen to what you and I have to say. Twelve nice people who are going to know that little kids like you can't make up stories like yours. Your are going to tell what happened and those twelve people are going to know that your are telling the truth.''

Remember, laughing and joking are important tools of the attorney's trade. Children are more comfortable with a relaxed approach.

## Voir Dire

Voir dire is a very important part in winning a child molestation case. First and foremost, parents who have reared their own children ought to be on the panel. Jurors whose children are a bit older than the victim should be favored. Such jurors can look back at their own children's development and recall that at such tender years, their own children had no concept of what one person can do with another sexually. As the old adage goes, you need not leave your common sense at home. Jurors who are parents, whether black or white, rich or poor, clever or stupid, will go into the jury room strongly disposed to vote for conviction.

Strong men often turn out to be the best jurors on this type of case. Nothing disgusts a healthy male like the victimization of a child. With women jurors, there is the risk that they have had incidents in their own childhood with "funny" uncles or neighbors. With these women, there is a chance that they will fail to see the intense emotional difference between what was, for them, a passing unpleasantness, and the totally destructive atmosphere in which this child has been forced to live. These same women may be aware that conviction may result in severe penalties. There are two choices one can make concerning potential weak jurors. Such a juror may be immediately excused, or the prosecutor may rely on final argument to educate and sway that juror. The deputy district attorney who chooses the latter had best be very good indeed at final argument.

The credibility of a child witness is somehow always more suspect than that of an adult, a peculiar and alarming fact. Having acknowledged this, the attorney should deal with the problem at the outset. The most effective way may be simply to ask if each juror is going to need more convincing from a child than from an adult.

"Have you or has anyone close to you ever been accused of such an action or crime?'' This ever-popular question has been part and parcel of our jury selection process of years. In fact, it is so old that many prosecutors forget to ask it. There seems to be even more of a tendency to shy away from the question in a case of this nature. Surprisingly enough, occasionally a juror will say, "My brother-in-law was accused of this by his step-daughter, but it turned out she was just jealous of him." The prosecutors response should be, "The People would like to thank and excuse . . . ."

The prosecutor should also be wary of elderly jurors. Jurors whose own children have already left home, established households of their own, and raised children, frequently adhere to the theory that although the activity is repugnant, children are absolutely subject to their parents. Older jurors who would unhesitatingly do great bodily injury to anyone who touched an unrelated child often grant immunity to in-home molesters.

The following are some suggested voir dire questions that will both educate the jury and be of assistance in revealing the jurors' biases and prejudices:

1. Do you naturally tend to question the credibility of small children or do you think children, in general, are less credible than adults?

2. Do you enjoy the company of children?

3. Do you feel that it would be impossible for you to find a person guilty in a case where it is one person's word against another?

4. Do you have any hearing problems? (In the courtroom, children tend to speak softly.)

5. This little girl is going to say some shocking things. Do you think that unpleasant as it may be for you to listen, that you will be able to listen to what she has to say?

6. Some people tend to view molestation of children within the family as a family affair and one that the government should leave in the family. Do you feel that it is proper for the police and the courts to interfere in this kind of a dysfunctional family?

7. Penalty plays no part in jury deliberations. The final disposition of this case will be in the hands of the judge. Are you confident that you could leave any thoughts of penalty or treatment out of your deliberation?

8. The child in this case is going to use words like "dick and "peter." Those are her words. Will you be able to listen to that kind of language, which is the only language she has for describing body parts? (With this state-ment/question, two purposes have been served. First, the juror must

answer with a verbal yes or no, and the body language that goes with the answer. Secondly, the prosecutor has used the words first, thereby preparing the juror for this verbiage.)

9 . There are some people who simply refuse to recognize the fact that children are sexually molested. Are you one of these people? (To this question, one juror responded, "No, I know it happens. I read it in the paper. Whenever I see an article like that, I just say to my wife, 'Thank God it doesn't happen in Lodi.' ")

All questions propounded to the jury should educate them. Inappropriate jurors will make themselves known quickly. They are the ones who demonstrate that they don't care for children, or that they have little or no empathy for children. They are the ones who find it possible to treat children as objects or property. They are the ones who feel that government has no business interfering in the family. Voir dire should cover the weaknesses of your case. Question in such a way to get each juror's assurance that, in spite of those weaknesses, if they believe the child beyond a reasonable doubt, they will vote guilty. The following are some examples of weaknesses commonly found in child molest cases and voir dire questions that will result in defusing the potentially devastating impact of those weaknesses.

1.  **Weakness:** Mother of victim met molester in bar and brought him home the first night she met him.
    **Question:** Can you assure us that even if you disapprove of a witness' lifestyle, your disapproval won't cause you to automatically disbelieve that witness?

2.  **Weakness:** Victim told no one about molests for many years.
    **Question:** In this case, if the evidence reveals that the child did not report these molests to anyone for several years, would you automatically disbelieve that the molests did not happen? You realize, of course, that there can be many reasons why a child would be unable to break the conspiracy of silence that surrounds these kinds of cases, don't you?
    You'll take into consideration, the *reasons* the child had for not reporting in judging the facts of this case, won't you?

Many jurors will help educate fellow jurors by such comments as, "I think it would be the exception rather than the rule that a molest victim would immediately complain." *Use* jurors such as these to further educate the other prospective jurors about child sexual abuse. For example, in most child molest cases, at least one juror will admit to having been sexually abused as a child. The defense attorney will obviously excuse these jurors, so enlist their services while you can. If they are not too embarrassed to talk about their experiences in front of the other jurors, ask questions that will bring home your crucial points. For example:

> **Question:** Did you ever report your molest? (90% will answer no) Did your failure to report have anything to do with a distrust of law enforcement? You realize then, of course, that just because a child does not report, doesn't mean that it didn't happen — or — did your molester ever accuse you of lying when you finally got the courage to tell?

3. **Weakness:** No corroboration to child's testimony. **Question:** If his honor instructs you that in a case of this sort, no corroboration of the victim's word is required, could you follow that law? You realize that sex crimes are rarely committed with eyewitnesses present or cameras rolling, don't you? Do you believe that children are entitled to protection under the law, just as adults are? So, in this case, if the evidence boils down to the word of a 4-year-old child and THAT'S ALL THE EVIDENCE THERE IS OF THE CRIMES but you believe that child beyond a reasonable doubt, how would you vote?

It is absolutely imperative to get each prospective juror's assurance that even without corroboration, they can convict based *solely* on the work of a child. Voir dire in such a way as to enable each juror to see that the rule of law which requires no corroboration in such cases is not only sensible, but essential for the protection of our children. Use this line of questioning even in cases where corroboration exists. In your closing argument, you can then remind the jurors that they promised to vote guilty based solely upon the word of a believable child. Then point out that not only have you presented the testimony of a child worthy of belief, but you have also provided evidence in corroboration.

4. **Weakness:** Victim molested previously by someone other than your defendant. (In most cases a motion *in limine* would be wise to keep this out of evidence, but if the motion is unsuccessful, it is best to voir dire on its impact.)
   **Question:** In this case, if the evidence shows that the victim was

previously molested by someone other than the accused, would that cause you automatically to disbelieve that she was molested by this man?

5.  **Weakness:** Defendant is very good looking or otherwise sympathetic. **Question:** Is there anything about the defendant's appearance occupation/etc. which causes you to believe that he could not have committed the crimes with which he's accused? Do you agree that you can't tell a book by its cover? Do you believe that there exists any class of people who are above suspicion when it comes to crimes of this sort? e.g., the defendant is a teacher. Do you believe that teachers (doctors, bankers, military men, professional athletes, Boy Scout leaders, etc.) are incapable of committing such crimes?

## Opening Statement

The opening statement allows the prosecutor to prepare the jury for a shock. Very few people are prepared to listen to a small child describe sex acts. While a little shock may be a valuable tool, too great a shock may result in the members of the jury tuning out the information — a form of emotional overload.

The opening statement continues the education begun in voir dire. In almost all cases, the child is the whole show, and the jury should be informed of this. They should be told so on voir dire, and they should be told so again in the opening statement. They should be informed that the entire case rests upon whether or not they, as the triers-of-fact, believe this child. The jury should be made aware that this is the heart of the case.

The purpose of the opening statement is to give a brief overview of the case, what the People intend to prove, and how they intend to prove it. In the opening statement you should inform the members of the jury that although such an outline will be attempted, the child is the final reporter of the events, and that it is her version and her credibility that are at issue, not the accuracy with which she fits her story into the prosecutor's outline. Be cautious; do not claim more than you will be able to prove.

Jurors should not be spared the colorful language the child will use. These graphic words should be presented to the jury matter-of-factly. The jury members must be forewarned that an eight-year-old child is going to take the witness stand and tell them what went on between herself and her stepfather in the only words she knows.

# CHILDREN'S STORY

"Ellen will tell you that on this occasion when she was taken to the master bedroom, she was told to take her clothes off. She will then tell you that Eddie rubbed her 'pee pee.' Those are her words for genitalia. She will also indicate, by pointing, that a person's 'pee pee' is located between the legs. Ellen will then go on to tell you that Eddie would take his clothes off and make her rub his pee pee. She will go on to say that eventually Eddie would stick his penis in Ellen's mouth and ejaculate. Of course, Ellen doesn't know the word 'ejaculate,' so she will tell you that 'white, yukky stuff came out of the end of it,' and sometimes she would have to swallow it."

The subject must be dealt with opening and honestly. The words aren't bad, the acts are. An embarrassed and hesitant prosecutor will infect the jury with the hesitancy and embarrassment. An open and honest prosecutor will produce an open and honest jury.

Experience has shown that emotional appears in the opening statement are usual unproductive. Jurors come into the courtroom laden with anger and disgust at the very idea of child molestation. Emotion, anger and disgust are the coin of the realm. But that anger and disgust are, almost without exception, based on misinformation. The job of the prosecutor in opening statement is go give the jury the education which is needed to spend that currency profitably.

The opening statement allows you to set the emotion and factual stage. Voir dire and opening statement are the first two steps in the education of the jury. The subject of sexual molestation of children, repugnant as it may be, is interesting, even gruesomely fascinating, and the jury will listen closely as the prosecutor shares education, interest, and concern with them.

## Case-In-Chief

A one-on-one case is a short case. The child (with the prosecutor's help) must carry the day. On the rare occasion when corroborating evidence exists, the prosecutor may see heaven. Medical evidence, photographs, and eye witnesses are welcome additions to any case. Such evidence graphically depicts the horridness of the crime. Some cases may be encountered where the child's genital area is actually mutilated or deformed as a result of the molestation. It is not hard to image the damage that can be wrought by an erect adult penis to the vagina of a tiny eleven-year-old. In one case, the doctor had no hesitation in testifying, "She was ripped and torn. The entrance to her vagina was mutilated." The doctor testified in a similar fashion about the trauma observed to the rectum of a sodomized seventeen-month-old child. The case had pictures for the jury's viewing. Corroboration need not be as dramatic as that, but if available, any corroboration should by all means be put before the jury. The doctor may be able to testify to nothing more than an abraded area around the vaginal opening, which in his opinion, would be consistent with a vigorous rubbing of that area. The defense will, of course, ask if that abraded area would not also be consistent with vigorous masturbation, or with failure to care for personal hygiene. The physician/witness will undoubtedly say, "yes." But then, on redirect, the prosecutor can come back with, "Would that abraded area also be consistent with a penis being rubbed back and forth between the legs?"

Spontaneous statements and fresh complaints by a child to another person are admissible in many circumstances. If the child told her grandmother about being molested on the day the incident occurred, the statement should be admissible. While the complaint in and of itself may seem a small thing, small things are about all the corroboration one can expect in most molestation cases. A spontaneous statement or a recent complaint negates the common defense tactic by attempting to make it appear that the child made this story up at some later time for some dark reason known only to her and the defense attorney.

Inconsistencies between the preliminary examination testimony of the child and the testimony at trial often abound. There are often inconsistencies in any witness's testimony between the preliminary examination and the trial. For a child, the nine or ten months between the preliminary examination and the trial (not to mention the time elapsed between the incidents described and the actual trial) represents at least one tenth of the child's entire life. One tenth of the life of a forty-year-old is four years. While it is certainly possible for a forty-year-old to recall significant events four years in the past, those events certainly are not recalled with the clarity which is possible immediately after they occurred. Similarly, a ten-year-old will not recall events of nine months previous with the same accuracy she would have had following the events. The prosecutor must concede such inconsistencies in the opening statement and explain them in the final argument.

Tempting though it may be, the prosecutor should give up any fantasies about having an expert testify about the child molestation paradigm. While child abuse is now a medically and legally recognized area of expertise, the child molestation paradigm is not. Experts on normal child development may be useful in explaining to the trier-of-fact the limitations, linguistically and cognitively of a child of a certain age. Such expertise may help the trier-of-fact separate competence and credibility. Experts can also be used to dispel the common misconceptions which may interfere with the ability to judge the case fairly, such misconceptions as are noted in Chapter II, "Fiction."

Experts, good investigation and a knowledge of the law are all, of course, necessary components of prosecution. Witnesses are also evidence. Too often, the courts and prosecutors treat witnesses as no more than items of evidence. Witnesses are special evidence. Being human, as we certainly hope they are, they should be treated with respect and care. Children are disadvantaged witnesses.

We would not expect a blind witness to describe a painting or a deaf witness to describe a symphony. A child cannot be expected to describe experiences with adult language and understanding. Advocates for children ask only that children be recognized as having special needs. Unless these special needs are recognized and addressed, the court room is an inaccessible arena to a child. A courtroom should offer justice to all.

### Defense

The defense generally falls into one of three categories:

1.  If didn't happen;

2.  There was touching, but it was only for benign purposes;

3.  The SODDI defense (*Some Other Dude Done It*).

If the defense is that the events never occurred, then the defense will invariably call the defendant to the stand. In cross-examining the defendant, you should keep in mind the type of individual with whom you are dealing. Many offenders tend to be obsequious and passive. They seek to ingratiate themselves to the jury. Juries are generally put off by cross-examination which attempts to tear such a mild-mannered person apart. The jury doesn't know, yet, that these mannerisms are indicative of one form of a child molestation pattern. They are going to find that out in the education provided by the final argument.

Cross-examination, like all other aspects of trial work, is a matter of individual style, but a calm, deliberate approach has proven most effective. The defendant should be questioned courteously, but in great detail about each of the events to which the child has testified. Detailed questions concerning the happenings of the day in question should be asked. Pin the defendant down to as many details as possible. After he has carefully denied or explained away each of the events, he should then be given the opportunity to explain to the jury how this little girl knows so much about sexual details. He should be asked about every sexual detail described by the child. The defendant's answers to these questions will probably fall into the category of "I don't know" or "she messed around with the neighborhood boys." If the defendant has spent time trying to convince the jury that he was a good guardian of the child, he should be able to explain to the jurors where in the world she got this detailed and sordid information. He should be asked if he has any indication what motive the child might have for making his life miserable. Either he will have no explanation, or the explanation will be that he punished her and she is trying to get back at him, or that she has some other mean-minded reason for torturing him. In any event, cross-examination can end with, "How did this seven-year-old child come up with this particular story? How did this child learn all of this sexual information?"

Along with the defendant's testimony, the defense will occasionally bring in character witnesses. "Have you ever seen the defendant with children?" Of course, the character witness will reply in the affirmative. Almost invariably, the character witness will describe acts and conduct that fit right into the child molestation paradigm. The character witness will describe a close relationship featuring the over-protectiveness and over-attentiveness which is so common among child molesters. If the defense position is that the defendant did, in fact, touch the child, but that he did so only for medicinal or hygienic reasons, the line of attack alters slightly. Not infrequently the defendant will adopt this defense. "Janie had a bad rash in her genital area, so I rubbed Vaseline on it. I was only trying to help. Her mother refused to do anything about it." If the defendant favors this defense, he has opened the door to priors. If the defendant has any similar prior conduct, that conduct can now be brought in since he has put his "intent" in issue.

A far less frequent defense is for the defendant to admit that something of an unusual nature happened to the child, but to point the finger of blame on another. The SODDI defense generally rears its head when there is corroborative medical testimony. If a doctor testifies that, "The child's vaginal area was mutilated," and that, "mutilation was consistent with an adult penis entering a small, undeveloped vagina," then the defense is hard pressed to deny that something happened to this child. There is generally some opinion offered by the defendant to explain the injuries away. Explanation sometimes takes the form of blaming it on the child. "She masturbated all the time. She must have done it herself." At other times, the explanation is accident. "She had an accident on her bike a few days ago. She must have gotten that injury then." Or the explanation is an attempt to blame another. Defendants in this type of action are frequently loathe to name the "other dude." Naming the "other dude" tends to make the "other dude" very cranky. Instead of flatly identifying the other person as the perpetrator, the more frequent defense is to weave a tapestry filled with other possible molesters. Evidence which raises only a mere possibility that some other person committed the crime is inadmissable under Evidence Code section 352. The prosecution should request a hearing in chambers.

## Final Argument

No one should presume to tell anyone else how to give a final argument. Argument, above all else, is a matter of style — ,and styles are as varied as individuals. Good argument possess three virtues — it should be creative, persuasive, and educational. Final argument is the last opportunity to educate the jury. Jurors are their own best experts. The ladies and gentlemen of the jury have all had experiences with children which are lingering in the back of their collective minds, waiting to be recalled.

There are several points to be made. The jurors are asked to remember that a child couldn't possibly make up a story like this. They are asked to remember that small children do not know sexual details. They are reminded that, although children do lie, they do not do it well, and that it is difficult for them to tell a coherent, made-up-story. The prosecutor takes the facts of the case and discusses them in the light of his own expertise.

"Ladies and gentlemen, we have here a classic example of the child molestation paradigm. We have heard testimony that this eight-year-old girl was left alone on a regular basis with her stepfather. Stepdaddy apparently leaped at this opportunity to assume custodial status. One wonders why. We would all like to believe that his motivation was caring and nurturing the child.

However, the truth of the matter is that his motives were selfish and perverted.

"You had an opportunity to observe the man here in the courtroom. He is a very passive man. Passivity is a common characteristic of child molesters. The child molesting man is fearful of relationships with adult women, so he has turned his attentions to a small child who certainly poses no great threat. What does a child molester look like? He looks like anyone else, and he *is* this man sitting before you today. He is this quiet, passive man who can only assert his masculinity with a small, defenseless child.

"This little girl did not make this story up. How many eight-year-old girls know that penises go from being flaccid to being erect, that penises ejaculate and that rubbing and sucking have these results? This little girl was clearly the victim of the acts you have heard her describe. No child, no matter how precocious, could fabricate a tale of this nature. The normal child's experiences are not broad enough to give rise to such credible and accurate testimony.

"The victimization of the child does not stop with the cessation of the molesting acts. This man has left an indelible mark on this child. Children from happy and supporting families grow up expecting happiness and support, therefore generally find happiness and support. This child has experienced manipulation and abuse. She will reach adulthood forever questioning the motives of those who are closest to her."

"This man wants you, the jury, to further victimize her by telling her that she is a liar. When you find this man guilty of the offenses charged, you will be giving this child a platform of trust on which she can try to rebuild her life."

"Unhappy and self-destructive adults do not spring from a vacuum. They come from unhappy and destructive homes. If we ever hope to break the cycle, we must start now. You must tell this man and all others that society will not allow him to commit such a grievous crime — the robbing of a child's innocence and security."

**Nowhere will differing philosophies in child molestation become more**

apparent than at sentencing. The strict constructionists can demand the upper term and be assured that this punishment is commensurate with the crime. Molesters have a profound and lasting effect on the child. However, for those DA's offices that favor a more creative approach, a variety of options are available, depending upon facilities and programs in the area.

Some jurisdictions favor pre-complaint diversion. Diversion programs carefully screen applicants to determine the likelihood of success in a predetermined treatment program. Some of the criteria for acceptance are: a steady job, long-term ties with the community, a good reputation in the community, and a fervent desire to solve the molesting problem as evidenced by an early and remorseful confession. Before acceptance into the program, the defendant *must* sign a full confession. He is made fully aware that state prison is the alternative to successful completion of the program, and that failure in the program will result in immediate reinstatement of criminal proceedings at which is confession will be admissable. The program, itself, lasts many years and includes group and individual therapy for the offender, the spouse, and the child.

Some jurisdictions make a similar sort of counseling a condition of probation, whether felony or misdemeanor. Those defendants who receive the benefit of such probation are once again made fully aware that state prison or county jail is the sword that hangs over their heads.

This clear understanding on the part of the defendant that failure in the program is deemed to be failure on probation has a demonstrated tendency to motivate the defendant to work in therapy. Good therapy in the field of sexual molestation is extremely painful. Therapy is so painful, in fact, that only the spectre of incarceration will keep most offenders in the program.

Many other programs for dealing with offenders exist. Other alternatives can surely be devised. Instituting a program designed to keep sexual molesters out of prison and yet protect children is certainly a commendable undertaking, but any such program should be undertaken only after careful planning and study of already-existing programs. The tendency to rush ill-conceived programs into practice in order to keep families together and off welfare is a grievous and lasting error. Society should be willing to support the family in order to protect the child.

# JURY TRIAL

# VI.    SUGGESTED READINGS

## PHYSICAL ABUSE OF CHILDREN

California commission on Crime Control and Violence Prevention. (1981) *An ounce of prevention: Toward an understanding of the causes of violence (Preliminary report to the people of California.* Sacramento, CA: California Commission on Crime Control and Violence Prevention.

Garbarino, J.,& Gilliam, G. (1980). *Understanding Abusive Families.* Lexington Books

Garbarino, J., & Sherman, D. (1980). (1980). High-risk families and high-risk neighborhoods. *Child Development, 51,* 188-198.

Gelles, R.J., & Cornell, C.P. (Eds.). (1985). *Intimate violence in families.* Beverly Hills, CA: Sage Publications.

Gil, D.G. (1970). Violence against children: Physical abuse in the United States. Cambridge, MA: Harvard University Press.

Kempe, C.H., Silverman, F.N., Steele, B.F., Droegemueller, W., & Silver, H.K. (1962). The battered-child syndrome. *Journal of the American Medical Association, 181,* 17-24.

Kempe, C.H., & Helfer, R.E. (1980). *The battered child (3rd ed.).* Chicago: University of Chicago Press.

Miller, A. (1983). *For Your own good: Hidden cruelty in child-rearing and the roots of violence.* (H. Hannum & H. Hannum, Trans.). New York: Farrar, Straus, Giroux.

Newburger, E.H. (Ed.). (1982). *Child abuse.* Boston: Little Brown.

# SUGGESTED READINGS

Straus, M.A. (1983). Ordinary violence, child abuse, and wife beating: What do they have in common? In D. Finkelhor, R.J. Gelles, G.T. Hotaling, & M.A. Straus (Eds.), *The dark side of families: Current family violence research* (pp. 213-234). Beverly Hills, CA: Sage Publications.

## CHILD NEGLECT

National Center on Child Abuse and Neglect. (1980). *Selected readings in child neglect*. (DHEW Publication No. OHDS 80-30253). Washington, DC: U.S. government Printing Office.

Polansky, N.A., DeSaix, C., & Sharlin, S. (1972). *Child Neglect: Understanding and reaching the parent*. New York: Child Welfare League of America.

Polansky, N.A., & Polansky, D. (1976). *Profile of neglect*. Washington, DC: Department of Health and Welfare.

## EMOTIONAL ABUSE

Asline, V.M. (1964). *Dibs in search of self*. New York:

Baily, T.F., & Baily, W. (1986). *Operational definitions of child emotional maltreatment (Final report of a federal-state project)*. (Available from Emotional Maltreatment Project Bureau of Social Services, Maine Department of Social Services, Station 11, 221 Main Street, Augusta, ME 04333)

Fortin, P.J., & Reed, S.R. (1984). Diagnosing and responding to emotional abuse within the helping system. *Child Abuse and Neglect. 8*(1), 117-119.

Garbarino, J., & Garbarino, A.C. (1980). *Emotional maltreatment of children*. Chicago: National Committee for Prevention of Child Abuse.

Garbarino, J., Gutman, E., & Seeley, J.W. (1986). *The psychologically battered child*. San Francisco: Jossey Bass.

# CHILDREN'S STORY

## CHILD SEXUAL ABUSE

Bresee, P., Sterns, G., Bess, B., & Packer, L. (1986). Allegations of child sexual abuse in child custody disputes: A therapeutic assessment model. *American Journal of Orthopsychiatry, 56*(4).

Burgess, A., Groth, A.N., Holmstrom, L., & Sgroi, S. (Eds.) (1978). *Sexual Assault of children and adolescents*. Lexington, MA: Lexington Books.

Butler, S. (1978). *Conspiracy of silence*. San Francisco: Volcano Press, Inc.

Corwin, D., Berliner, L., Goodman, G., Goodwin, J., & White, S. (1987). Child sexual abuse and custody disputes. Journal of Interpersonal Violence. Vol.2, No.1.

Finkelhor, D. (1979). *Sexually victimized children*. New York: Free Press.

Finkelhor, D. (1980). Risk factors in the sexual victimization of children. *Child Abuse & Neglect, 4*, 265-273.

Finkelhor, D. (Ed.). (1984) *Child sexual abuse: New theory and research*. New York: Free Press.

Finkelhor, D. (Ed.). (1986). *A sourcebook on child sexual abuse*. Beverly Hills, CA: Sage Publications.

Forward, S., & Buck, C. (1979), *Betrayal of innocence: Incest and its devastation*. New York: Penguin Books.

Herman, J. (1981). *Father-daughter incest*. Cambridge, MA: Harvard University Press.

James, B. & Nasjleti, M. (1983). *Treating sexual abused children and their families*. Palo Alto, CA: Consulting Psychologist Press, Inc.

Jones, D.P. (1986). Reliable and fictitious accounts of sexual abuse in children. *Journal of Inter-Personal Violence, 2*.

# SUGGESTED READINGS

Kempe, R.S., & Kempe, C.H. (1984). *The common secret: Sexual abuse of children and adolescents*. New York: W.H. Freeman.

MacFarlane, K., Waterman, J., Conerly, S., Damon, L., Durfee, M., & Long, S. (1986). *Sexual abuse of young children: Evaluation and Treatment*. New York: Guilford Press.

Meiselman, K.C. (1978). *Incest*. San Francisco: Jossey Bass Publishers.

Rush, F. (1980). *The best kept secret*. New York: Prentice-Hall.

Russell, D. (1980). *The secret trauma: Incest in the lives of girls and women*. New York: Basic Books.

Sgroi, S.M. (Ed.). (1983). *Handbook of clinical intervention in child sexual abuse*. Lexington Books.

Summit, R.C. (1983). The child abuse accommodation syndrome. *Child Abuse & Neglect*, 7, 177-193.

Weisberg, D.K. (1985). *Children of the night: A study of adolescent prostitution*. Lexington, MA: Lexington Books.

## RESPONDING TO THE ABUSED CHILD

Davis, D. (1986). *Working with children from violent homes: Ideas and techniques*. Santa Cruz, CA: Network Publications.

Eth, S., & Pynoos, R.S. Developmental perspectives on psychiatric trauma in childhood. In C.R. Figley (Ed.), *Trauma and its wake: The study and treatment of post-traumatic stress disorder*. (pp. 36-52). New York: Brunner/Mazel.

Faller, K.C. (Edl). (1981). *Social work with abused and neglected children*. New York: Free Press.

# CHILDREN'S STORY

Gil, E.M. (1982). *Foster parenting abused children*. Chicago: National Committee on Child Abuse Prevention.

Groth, A. N., & Stevenson, Jr., T.M. (1984). *Anatomical drawings for use in the investigation and intervention of child sexual abuse*. Newton Centre, MA: Forensic Mental Health Associates.

Johnson & Foley (1984). Differentiating fact from fantasy: The reliability of children's memory. *Journal of Social Issues, 40* (33).

Jones, D.P.H., & McQuiston, M. (1985). *Interviewing the sexually abused child*. Denver, CO: C. Henry Kempe National Center for Preventing and Treating Child Abuse and Neglect.

Loftus & Davies (1984). Distortions in the memory of children. *Journal of Social Issues, 40*(51).

Mann, E., & McDermott, Jr., J.F. (1983). Play therapy for victims of child abuse and neglect. In C.E. Schaefer and K.J. O'Connor (Eds.), Handbook of play therapy (281-307). New York: John Wiley & Sons.

Martin, H.P. (Ed.). (1976) *The abused child: A multidisciplinary approach to developmental issues and treatment*. Cambridge, MA: Ballinger.

Terr, L.C. (1983). Play therapy and psychic trauma: A preliminary report. In C.E. Schaefer and K.J. O'Connor (Eds.), *Handbook of play therapy* (281-307). New York: John Wiley & Sons.

Wohl, A., & Kaufman, B. (1985). *Silent screams and hidden cries: An interpretation of artwork by children from violent homes*. New York: Brunner Mazel.

## CHILD ABUSE AND CRIMINAL JUSTICE

Benedek, E., & Schetky, D. (1985). Allegations of sexual abuse in child custody and visitation disputes. *Emerging Issues in Child Psychiatry and the Law*. Schetky & Benedek (Eds.). New York, NY: Bruner/Mazel.

# SUGGESTED READINGS

Berliner & Barbieri (1984). The testimony of the child victim of sexual assault. *Journal of Social Issues*, *40*(125).

Burgess, A.W., & Holmstrom, L.L. (1978). The child and family during the court process. In A.W. Burgess, A.N. Groth, L.L. Holmstrom, & S.M. Sgroi (Eds.), *Sexual assault of children and adolescents*. (205-230). Lexington, MA: Lexington Books.

Duquette, D.N. (1980). Liberty and lawyers in child protection. In C.H. Kempe, & R.E. Helfer (Eds.), *The battered child (3rd ed.)*. Chicago: University of Chicago Press.

Eatman, R., & Buckley, J. (1986). Protecting child victim/ witnesses. American Bar Association.

Goldstein, J., Freud, A., & Solnet, A.J. (1973). *Beyond the best interest of the child*. New York: Free Press.

Goldstein, S. (1976). *The sexual exploitation of children: A practical guide to assessment, investigation, and intervention*. New York: Elsevier Science Publishing.

Goodman (1984). Children's testimony in historical perspective. *Journal of Social Issues*, *40*(9).

Goodman, G.S. (Ed.). (1984). The child witness. *Journal of Social Issues*, *40* (2).

Goodman & Helgeson (1985). Child sexual assault: Children's memory and the law. *University of Miami Law Review*, *40*(181).

Green, A.H. (1986). True and false allegations of sexual abuse in child custody disputes. *Journal of the American Academy of Child Psychiatry and the Law*, *25*(4).

Howell, J.N. (1980). The role of law enforcement in the prevention, investigation, and treatment of child abuse. In C.H. Kempe, & R.E. Helfer (Eds.), *The battered child (3rd ed.)*. Chicago: University of Chicago Press.

# CHILDREN'S STORY

Marin, Holmes, Guth & Kova (1975). The potential of children as eyewitnesses: A comparison of children and adults on eyewitnesses tasks. *Law and Human Behavior, 3*(295).

Melton, G. (1981). Children's competency to testify. *Law and Human Behavior, 5*(73).

Melton, G., Bukley, J., & Wulkan, D. (1981). Competency of children as witnesses. *Child Sexual Abuse and the Law*, pp. 125-126. National Legal Resource Center for Child Advocacy and Protection, American Bar Association Review.

Schuman, D.C. (1986). False accusations of physical and sexual abuse. *American Academy of Psychiatric Law, 14*(1).

Whitcomb, D., Shapiro, E., & Stellwagen, L. (1985). When the victim is a child. Government Printing Office.

## ADULT SEX OFFENDERS

Abel, C.G., Becker, J.V., Cuningham-Rather, J., Rouleau, J., Kaplan, M., & Reich, J. (1984). *The treatment of child molesters: A manual.* (Available from authors through Columbia University, 722 West 168th Street, Box 17, New York, NY 10032).

Abel, C.G., Becker, J.V., Cunningham-Rathner, J., & Murphy, W.D. (1987). Self-reported sex crimes of nonincarcerated paraphiliacs. *Journal of Interpersonal Violence, 2*(1), 3-25.

Carnes, P. (1983). *The sexual addiction*. Minneapolis: Compcare Publications.

Greer, J.G., & Stuart, I.R. (Eds.). (1983). *The sexual aggressor: Current perspectives on treatment*. New York: Van Nostrand Reinhold.

Groth, A.N. (1979). *Men who rape: the psychology of the offender*. New York: Plenum Press.

# SUGGESTED READINGS

Groth, A.N. & Birnbaum, B. (1978). Adult sexual orientation and attraction to underaged persons. *Archives of Sexual Behavior*, 7, 175-181.

Groth, A.N. & Burgess, A.W. (1977). Motivational intent in the sexual assault of children. *Criminal Justice and Behavior*, 4(3), 253-264. Knopp, F.H. (1984). *Retraining adult sex offenders: Methods and models*. Syracuse, NY: Safer Society Press.

## YOUTHFUL SEX OFFENDERS

Becker, J.V., Cunningham-Rathner, J., & Kaplan, M.S. (1986). Adolescent sexual offenders: Demographics, criminal and sexual histories, and recommendations for reducing future offenses. *Journal of Interpersonal Violence*, 1(4), 431-445.

Becker, J.V., Kaplan, M.S., Cunningham-Rather, J., & Kavoussi, R. (1986). Characteristics of adolescent incest perpetrators: Preliminary finding. *Journal of Family Violence*, 1(1), 85-96.

Agee, V.L. (1979). *Treatment of the violent incorrigible adolescent*. Lexington, MA: Lexington Books.

Deisher, R.W., Wenet, G.A., Paperny, D.M., Clark, T.F., & Fehrenbach, P.A. (1982). Adolescent sexual offense behavior: The role of the physician. *Journal of Adolescent Health Care*, 2(4) 279-286.

Gil, E. (1987). *Children who molest: A guide for parents of Young Sex Offenders*. Walnut Creek, CA: Launch Press

Groth, A.N., & Loredo, C.M. (1981). Juvenile sexual offenders: Guidlines for assessment. *International Journal of Offender Therapy and Comparative Criminology*, 25(1), 31-39.

Groth, A.N., Hobson, W.F., Lucey, K.P., & St. Pierre, J. (1981). Juvenile sexual offenders: Guidlines for treatment. *International Journal of Offender Therapy and Comparative Criminology*, 25(3), 265-272.

# CHILDREN'S STORY

Heinz, J.W., Gargaro, S., & Kelly, K.G. (1987). *A model residential juvenile sex-offender treatment program: The Hennepin county home school.* Syracuse, NY: Safer Society Press.

Knopp, F.H. (1982). *Remedial intervention in adolescent sex offenses: Nine program descriptions.* Syracuse, NY: Safer Society Press.

Knopp, F.H. (1985). *The youthful sex offender: The rationale and goals of early intervention and treatment.* Syracuse, NY: Safer Society Press.

Lafond, M., Thomas, P., & Stark, W. (1981). Group therapy with adolescent sex offenders in a state juvenile correction institution. (Available from authors through Echo Glen Children's Center, 33010 S.E. 99th Street, Snoqualimie, WA).

Ryan, G. (Ed.). (1986). Interchange: A cooperative newsletter of the adolescent perpetrator network. (Available from the Adolescent Perpetrator Network, The C. Henry Kempe National Center for Preventing and Treating Child Abuse and Neglect, 1205 Oneida Street, Denver, CO 80220).